C000203185

PEACEHAVEN
A Pictorial History

The founder of Peacehaven, Mr. C. W. Neville. He was born in Darlington in 1881. His father, who was an exhibition promoter, had changed the family name from Ussher because the family disapproved of his marriage. His grandfather, Sir Thomas Ussher, had the distinction of accompanying Napoleon Bonaparte to his exile on the Isle of Elba.

While Charles was still a boy his family emigrated to Canada, but his father's sudden death left his mother in somewhat straightened circumstances and Charles was sent to live with relatives in Northern Ontario. He stayed there until he was sixteen and then ran away from home to Toronto where he 'put himself through college and university' and later started a newspaper which was quite successful.

Tiring of Toronto, which he regarded as being 'bigoted and churchified', he made his way to Australia where he went into partnership selling real estate. With his partner he bought a schooner called *The Snark* and sailed to New Guinea, taking a quantity of cheap trinkets. Observing that the island's river waters ran blue they discovered the presence of copper pyrites and purchased the mineral rights from the tribal chiefs with the trinkets.

Later he returned to Canada where he purchased land near the city of Regina, the capital of Saskatchewan. He divided the land up into plots and between 1910 and 1912 a considerable number of these were sold to mainly British and European settlers.

At the end of 1912 he returned to England, set up offices in Shaftesbury Avenue, London, and married Dorothy Rochard, with whom he eventually raised a family of two boys and a girl.

He died in Rottingdean in 1960.

PEACEHAVEN
A Pictorial History

Bob Poplett

Phillimore

1993

Published by
Phillimore and Co. Ltd.,
Shopwyke Manor Barn, Chichester, West Sussex

© Bob Poplett, 1993

ISBN 0 85033 880 8

Printed and bound in Great Britain by
BIDDLES LTD.,
Guildford, Surrey

List of Illustrations

Frontispiece: The founder of Peacehaven, Mr. C. W. Neville

Acknowledgements

I wish to say thank you to the many people who have helped me compile the contents of this book, especially the following: Christine Hanson at Phillimore; Peacehaven Town Council; Lewes District Council; East Sussex County Council; Mr. Davey, County Archivist; Public Records Office Kew; Tangmere Military Aviation Museum; John Mathias; Alan Green; Pat Poplett; *Peacehaven Post* (1921-26); the *Gazette*; the *Advertiser*; the *Record*; *Downland Post* (Magazine and Review); *Peacehaven and Newhaven Times* (1946); *Sussex Daily News* (1936); and not least of all thank you to Mr. Roderick Neville (son of C.W.N.) and Mr. Bob Copper, the well known Rottingdean author.

Foreword

No-one visiting Peacehaven for the first time today could possibly imagine the colourful and controversial nature of its early history. The neat and tidy aspect of its paved and grass-verged avenues and its well-appointed homes gives no clue to the haphazard beginnings from which this orderliness has developed. Peacehaven had a difficult birth, and its very conception was daring if not dubious.

For untold centuries this part of the Sussex seaboard had been a deserted and rather bleak tract of downland exposed to all the buffetings of wind and weather off the sea. It was a landscape without figures save the lonely shepherd who bent his back to the wind, or the occasional traveller making his way along the cliff-top track between Brighton and Newhaven. But in 1914 the man to whom Peacehaven owes its existence drove his motorcar along this track, looked at the green expanse of turf open to the sea and the sky and saw at once the potential for a seaside development. He had a vision and dreamt of a garden city by the sea.

If its birth had been difficult, its infancy also had problems. Most of the earliest settlers came as the result of winning plots of land given as prizes in a competition organised through the national daily newspapers, but the procedures adopted led to acrimony and dispute. There were allegations of fraud and libel, recriminations and lawsuits in the High Courts of Justice. But, strangely enough, out of all this chaos the majority of the new residents themselves emerged without serious complaint.

On arrival they would throw a fence around their prize plots – and in some instances any adjoining ground they thought they might get away with – build a simple, sometimes ramshackle bungalow or shack, get a few chickens and a goat or two and proceed to live a spartan life comparable in many ways to that in the Australian out-back. Often their nearest neighbour would live a quarter of a mile away up the dirt road, but after life in the inner cities many of them looked upon it as a little Eden by the sea.

Memories of those days are now shared only by a handful of the older and longer-established residents, some of whom look back to the freedom and friendliness of that era of near-colonial life-style with affection. Therefore it is timely that this pictorial record of that era should be made available.

The whole of the Peacehaven story has unfolded within the span of a human lifetime, the great acceleration in building development and consequent explosive increase in population having taken place in the last thirty years. The story is probably not yet over but this book emphasises how far one man's dream has travelled up the long and rocky road towards achievement, and how far it has yet to go if it is ever to reach its goal and become a garden city by the sea.

Bob Poplett, who was one of the pioneer settlers, has written an informative and interesting introduction to the subject and has allowed photographs from his extensive and excellent collection to speak for themselves. Wisely is it said that one picture is worth a thousand words and they tell the story most eloquently.

BOB COPPER

Introduction

I feel privileged to be the custodian of a personal collection which recalls the unique history of Peacehaven. The many hundreds of pictures, plans, maps, written material and documents represent over 60 years of gathering items, which I suppose you could call my main hobby.

I was born in West London in 1916 and shortly afterwards my family moved to Rye Harbour. In 1923 we moved to Peacehaven and my parents were amongst the earliest settlers, truly pioneers in an area that mostly comprised open fields and few public amenities.

Our house, if you could call it that, was a wood and asbestos shack in Seaview Avenue, on the site of what is today Ron Young's Motor Engineering Yard. The dwelling, described as a holiday home, cost about £150 freehold and stood on two plots of land with a grass track for a road that was inpassable in wet weather. The structure was built from good secondhand 4 in. x 2 in. sawn timber – difficult to find at that time, as materials were still scarce in the aftermath of the First World War. The house was covered inside and out with flat asbestos sheets and a roof laid with felt under diamond-shaped asbestos tiles.

After two years of living in these primitive conditions, with no proper sanitation, the family moved. Our first Peacehaven home was let as a chicken run. Later my father bought a new house in Outlook Avenue, which was a great improvement. The brick-built dwelling became our home for six years until 1933.

My father had a fruit shop on the South Coast Road. I began with a haulage and general dealer's business, which was interrupted by the Second World War, as I received my call-up papers in March 1940. After being medically discharged a few years later I returned to Peacehaven with my wife, Flo. I bought a lorry and began an uphill struggle to restart the business, trying to make a living during a period when money and materials were in very short supply just after the war. The severe rationing of materials was to last another five years and, in many ways, these hardships echoed the plight of the district's earlier settlers after the First World War.

During the late 1940s, with the aid of a light lorry, I worked as a scrap metal merchant, breaking up small ships, fruit dealing, demolition work and buying war surplus stocks. Throughout those years I also had the opportunity to gather material on early Peacehaven. This included copies of the *Peacehaven Post*, and other publications, such as the rare plans and maps upon which the design of the town was based.

As the variety of mementos grew so did my interest in the filing and recording of Peacehaven's local history and it has been my privilege to have made many contacts amongst the settlers. I have always been conscious that a parish is not merely bricks and mortar, but the people who make up the neighbourhood.

In the early '20s there was a certain amount of 'Empire building' as people chose to endure living in an isolated area, in an environment not dissimilar to the places from where many colonials had returned to retire.

Due to some bad planning decisions a certain notoriety has dogged Peacehaven; it remains a subject for students in town planning to this day. Nevertheless the area had an attraction for many pioneers which they staunchly defended. This is easy to understand when taking into account the physical background, not least the incomparable chemistry of the cliff top and downland air.

I was fortunate to be a member of the former Peacehaven Council from 1951 and then of the newly created Town Council in the 1970s until 1991. Thus my historic involvement in the town was coupled with civic pride in my endeavours to foster the best interests of the area.

With its four-fold increase in population, and the growth in the town centre and surrounding estates during the last decade or so, the town has dramatically broken away from its old image of rigid grid-pattern roads and avenues with little of architectural interest.

But I like to think that the real Peacehaven, has foundations well and truly laid by those pioneering settlers, for the benefit of future generations, resulting in great community spirit.

Peacehaven's Founder
Mr. C. W. Neville was the founder of Peacehaven. The land, comprising various estates, was purchased between 1914-23 and encompassed the Downs from the east side of Rottingdean to the west side of Newhaven. It also stretched north around Telscombe village onto and abutting Dean's Farm, Piddinghoe, to the south side of the village, and then straddled the Lewes to Newhaven road as far as the river Ouse.

Neville controlled various companies, such as the Cavendish Land Co., The Peacehaven Estates Co., The Saltdean Estate Co., The South Coast Land and Resort Co., Peacehaven Building Supply Co., Peacehaven Electric Light Co., Peacehaven Water Co., St Margaret's Flats, Nell Gwynne House, Chelsea, *Tudor Close Hotel*, *Ocean Hotel*, Peacehaven Hotel Ltd., Peacehaven Building Society and many more.

For a number of years, especially during the 1920s, Peacehaven's progress was dominated by Mr. Neville. If the company agreed, it was agreed; if not, one was out on a limb. During the 1930s this position altered and local government assumed more control, although this was suspended by the Second World War. Peacehaven did not expand until 10 years later, when a variety of Town Planning Acts were implemented, bringing new and modern development, roads, sewers and services; all a far cry from 40 years previously.

Roderick Neville, writing from Italy, describes his father thus:

> My father was the pioneer founder of Peacehaven, the creation of this estate was the culmination of a successful career of land and estate development, covering many areas of England, Australia and Canada. This man truly had a vision, some will say perhaps before his time but time has proved him right, he fought for the co-operation of the local Authority's and at last this town now has its roads, sewers, services and facilities. Progress is now catching up with the clock, the team that helped him succeed were his right arm.
>
> It gives me great pleasure to commend to you a useful section of this town's history.
>
> I wish to record my best wishes and kindest regards to you, Bob Poplett, for your interest and devotion to Peacehaven over these many years.

March 1914
I would like to refresh your memory with what the late Mr. Charles Neville said, in his recollections printed in the *Downland Review* of 1959:

The first time I saw the land forming Peacehaven was in 1914. Now you might well ask how I came to be on the South Coast in 1914 and a landowner there shortly after, and the answer to this is a very simple one, but one which has had far reaching consequences. During 1913-15, I was living at Bexhill-on-Sea, and on a fine summer day early in 1914, my wife and I motored along the coast road to Brighton. In those days roads were not what they are today.

The road was fairly good up the west side of Eastbourne, but once on the Downs they were atrocious, just flinty tracks with deep ruts, along which the going was difficult and hard. On leaving Newhaven we climbed out of the town on the South Coast Road and on reaching the top of the hill just beyond where the Golf Club House now stands, we first saw the land which is now Peacehaven. It lay without a house upon it for a mile to the west with the exception of a toll house alongside the road which was situated where the Eastern Pylon of Peacehaven now stands. On the western side was Telscombe Cliffs with a few scattered houses and the Restaurant Post Office, which still stands there although it is no longer a post office. It did not take long to visualise this site as ideal for development as a seaside resort and I could not understand why someone had not previously realised its possibilities, but on going further we came up Telscombe Cliffs where an attempt at development had been made; but its derelict appearance showed that it had failed. After Telscombe Cliffs there was more open Downland which was Telscombe Tye and further on Saltdean, where the only inhabitants lived in five derelict cottages which at one time were occupied by the Coastguard Service and the Post Office at Telscombe Cliffs about a mile along the road. There are very few people now in the neighbourhood who can recollect the happenings of 1916-18.

The first real development on this part of the South Coast was at Telscombe Cliffs where the Cavendish Land Company had built the post office and less than a dozen houses. A well had been put down in the centre of the estate and two roads had been formed running about a quarter of a mile from the South Coast Road through the centre of the estate northwards. The manner in which the Cavendish Land Company had tried to popularise Telscombe Cliffs was by the old fashioned method of advertising an auction sale to be held on the ground on a certain day. No doubt a tent had been erected in which a free and plentiful supply of sandwiches and food and copious supplies of beer were available and when all were in a joyful and contented mood the auctioneer would mount his rostrum and open the proceedings by an eulogy of the estate and produce plans of the plots and would read out the conditions under which the plots would be sold for building purposes and no doubt, tell the would-be purchasers what developments and improvements were to be carried out. How the people got there I do not know, but years ago some old timers told me that most came down from London by train on free tickets or on a special train and that there was a line up of every kind of vehicle outside of Newhaven station which took the passengers to the Estate for 6d. and 1s. Fares from London to the South Coast about 1900 were at times as low as 2s. 6d. return and right up to the outbreak of the First World War fares were, on special occasions, almost as low. The regular return fare to Brighton was only 4s. or perhaps a little more to Eastbourne, Hastings and Newhaven. The Cavendish Land Company must have had considerable success over a period of years because, when we took over the Estate in 1923 or 1924, about one third of the plots had been sold, water was being pumped from the well supplying the scattered houses, but no improvements had been made beyond the two dirt roads, the well and a way had been made to the foreshore down the side of the cliff. This way, the well and the watertower house all long ago disappeared, but the roads remained and others were added later.

During 1915, I obtained possession of the land I had bought, and a number of surveyors and men were engaged, in a few months a good deal of land was laid out in accordance with the plan I had decided on and several thousand building sites were pegged out in plots 25 ft. x 100 ft., the usual size of a building plot in those days. What later became Peacehaven was a lonely and difficult place to reach, hours would go by without a vehicle appearing on the road and only then a farm cart or wagon. Later on there was an occasional bus with solid rubber tyres and frequent breakdowns. The first building to be erected was the asbestos hut which later became the Rosemary Dairy which was situated at the corner of Piddinghoe Avenue and the South Coast Road. I slept in that office for a good many months whilst the preliminary work was being done.

Yes, the original name of Peacehaven was 'New Anzac on Sea', a name chosen by the judges from more than 80,000 names submitted in a countrywide competition for a name for the new seaside resort. The advertisement appeared in all the national daily newspapers published at that time which were much as they are today, although I believe there were far more of them and their advertising rates were certainly far less than they are now. At that time I can remember that one could have a whole page in *The Times* for £200. The London office, from which the estate was advertised, was in Grays Inn Road, and we started with a very modest staff of four or five people. When our advertisement for the competition began to appear the entries began to roll in. I have not got a copy of the advertisement today, but they were generally a quarter of a page. The competition offered a first prize of £100 cash, and 50 of our regular size building sites priced at £50. There was a coupon for the competitors to fill out with the name they submitted for the estate and their own name and address. The advertisement ran over a period of about a month and my recollection is that I spent from two to three thousand pounds in advertising which was a pretty good amount to spend to obtain publicity in those days.

Competition brings in thousands of replies
Well, from a trickle, the replies and coupons came in by hundreds and then by thousands and to each we sent our advertising material inviting them to come and visit the Estate. Every day our staff had to be increased until near the end we had more than 30 assistants who were sorting coupons and writing envelopes sending out advertising matter. I had not expected such a great response although I had anticipated a goodly number of replies and towards the close of the competition we were almost swamped by the mail we received. In the last two days the Post Office were delivering a dozen bags of letters, containing coupons, at a time. Well, the sorting of those coupons was a job. We had a dozen assistants, who first went over them and roughly sorted them out, the names of similar kinds which had come in large quantities, were placed in boxes and set aside. There were several hundreds of names of different kinds which were of existing seaside resorts and these were at once set aside as impossible. In fact, there were, in many cases, several hundred of the same name, any of which would have been suitable for the purpose, but we could hardly divide the prize money among hundreds of people, so those names also had to be set aside. There were many excellent names suggested, but as there were so many of each kind, they also had to be discarded.

At that time 'Anzac' was a very popular name owing to the exploits of the Australians and New Zealanders at Gallipoli Peninsular, but there were too many of just 'Anzac', but in sorting the entries out we found just two with the name 'New Anzac on Sea', there were numerous 'Anzac on Sea' coupons and combinations of 'Anzac' but only two of the one kind and after more than a week's work of careful examination the judges finally decided to award the first and second prizes to 'New Anzac on Sea' and that became the well advertised name of the new resort.

Some time after this, representations were made to me that 'Anzac' (as a result of the tragic happenings at Gallipoli), was a word that should not be used to advertise a new seaside resort in England. With this I entirely agreed, and had always thought that some of the better names that had been sent in should be used for the purpose, but we were tied to finding a name which stood alone or almost so, and that is why the name was chosen. I afterwards saw both the contestants who had sent in the name and I was not impressed with either their intelligence or their personality for both took the prize money which was divided between them with blank faces and without giving a word of thanks to the donors. I think their own opinion of themselves was that they were very clever people. Six months or so after that, at a meeting held on the estate with the people who had won prize plots, it was agreed by unanimous consent that the name be changed to Peacehaven, a name that I also favoured and that I hope will be forever known.

It will, however, interest you to know that more than 200 people put forward the name 'Peacehaven' in the competition so that no one had a monopoly on it, but we still receive letters from people, and had one in 1959, from a person who sent in that name or claiming to have done so and asserting they were entitled to the first prize.

The initial steps taken to make Peacehaven a living reality had been defeated by the destruction of all that had been done through the advent of war and the use of the land comprising the estate for agricultural purposes. When the war came to an end and the estate had been released from control which was, as I recall, about 1920. By that time the South Coast Land and Resort Company had been formed by myself and others in order to proceed with the development of the estate, no time was lost in communicating with the thousands of people who had become owners of building sites and who were told that the sites they had purchased would be surveyed again and pegged out, and this was done. In fact the whole of the area between where the Pylons now stand was pegged out and the roads marked and set out and we started to erect some buildings.

Struggle for road making and building materials

Building material was almost impossible to obtain for two or three years following the end of the war and practically no house building was possible during that time, despite the outcry for homes from every quarter. There is, of course, no rock or stone on the South Downs suitable for road building, except for flint which is not the best material for that purpose and is difficult to obtain in quantity. There had been a war camp at Seaford so arrangements were made to buy a good many of the buildings, for the wood they contained, in addition to the material on the roads, all the water pipes in the ground and the electric cables and other material which could be used in connection with buildings. After looking over what we had bought we had more than one surprise; one of which occurred in the shape of a great drum of heavy electric cable which had never been openedand was buried in a pit that had been covered over by debris. At a later date the roll of cable proved very useful to the Peacehaven Electric Light and Power Company which we afterwards formed to supply light and power on the estate.

First to start after-war home building

Thousands of loads of road material were transported over from Seaford to make some of the metalled roads which were formed at that time. We started to build small houses and sold what material we had to others who were more than anxious to start building. They were small and indifferent houses and we only had material for about a dozen at that time, but these buildings at Peacehaven were, I believe, the very earliest to be built anywhere after the war. Some of them still stand and are homes to those who built them, and perhaps, when critics of Peacehaven voice their views, they will take these facts into consideration. We did at least provide homes for people to live in. When the materials became available building proceeded at a great pace. During the years following the war more and more people bought building sites and shops began to spring up along the South Coast Road. Now everyone at times makes mistakes and one of the greatest we made at that time was to set aside all of the plots facing the South Coast Road for shops. Too many were bought and built upon for this purpose and, as a result too many people opened shops in comparison to the population and in consequence some of these failed and their premises soon exhibited a derelict appearance. That was unfortunate for us and for Peacehaven but it did not stop the building of houses or the buying of land.

Now reverting to the early days, as growth went on we had to provide the amenities ourselves. We tried to get the Seaford and Newhaven Water Company to supply the estate with water, and to lay the necessary mains for that purpose, but the sum they demanded was exorbitant. Although they had a reservoir to the east and overlooking the Estate we had to find other sources of supply, so we formed the Peacehaven Water Company Limited and took over the plant which had been used to supply Telscombe Cliffs Estate in its early days and improved and extended its pumping capacity. We laid mains in the shape of two inch pipes and often one inch pipes along the side roads and succeeded in giving a water supply to each house which had been erected. After acquiring Saltdean lands we had an artesian well sunk to a depth of 300 ft. and then struck an underground stream running to the sea – it must have been such at that depth, the drill dropped 15 ft. and water rose up to 100 ft. of the surface. We built a half million gallon reservoir on the highest part of the estate and laid a six inch main from the well and used to supply, with the aid of diesel and electric pumps, half a million gallons a day with which Saltdean, Telscombe Cliffs and Peacehaven were supplied. This went on for several years and later I will tell you what happened to bring the Peacehaven Water Company to an end. We only had our new water supply ready in time because excessive pumping at Telscombe Cliffs had brought on an infiltration of sea water into the well and it had eventually to be closed down.

Providing electric light in 1924

Between the years 1920 and 1930 a great deal happened at Peacehaven. About 1924 we formed the Peacehaven Electric Light Company Limited. Its generating plant, consisting of three large diesel engines giving about 150 h.p., was situated at Peacehaven, close to the boundary of Telscombe Cliffs Estate, about 400 yards north of the South Coast Road. It gave an ample supply of electric light and power at that time, but the cost of generating was high, as were the charges for providing light. In about 1930 it was sold to the Southern Electric Company, and it was joined with that enterprise until it was taken into the National Grid system.

Creating what we needed

During this time we established and ran a sawmill and joinery works on a site south of the South Coast Road between Gladys and Sunview Avenues. During 1921-22 the *Peacehaven Hotel* was constructed, and it opened on 10 October 1922. We then formed a company to run it, which it did quite successfully for several years. This was a beautiful place when built and it was furnished sumptuously. The ornamental stonework fireplaces and doorways and the statuary which came from Italy were works of art, some of the original work is still there. On its opening day a grand luncheon was laid on, which was attended by many well-known people including Lord and Lady Teynham, Mrs. Dorothy Neville, Mr. John Waddington, J.P., Commander Graham, O.B.E., Captain Morris, Mr. W. Norman, J.P., Mr. A. H. G. Fokker, Mr. Van Bommal and Lt. Commander H. Perrin, Secretary of the Royal Aero Club, and 300 other invited guests, many of whom had come from London by a special Pullman Express train. Luncheon was served in a large marquee in the hotel grounds. The guests were received at the hotel main entrance by my wife and myself, and the Right Hon. Lord Teynham presided at the luncheon and was Chairman of the meeting which afterwards took place. We had a plant for making breeze blocks with modern machines at that time and a great number were made and sold not only at Peacehaven, but also sent elsewhere.

The Peacehaven Hotel

During this time Mr. A. Cripps was Works Manager on the estate – one of the old school – a perfectly honest and straightforward Sussex man who wanted a good day's work for the wage his men were paid, and got it. He was respected by all and one to whose credit a great deal is due for what he did at Peacehaven. There were many more local workers employed by the Company up to the outbreak of the Second World War and more than 15 of them had been continually with us for about 20 years.

In answer to a loyal message to King George V at Balmoral sent by the editor of *The Peacehaven Post* a telegram was received from the king thanking the inhabitants of Peacehaven for their message of loyalty to himself and members of the Royal Family, which he had been pleased to receive. The Band of the Royal Field Artillery played in the gardens during the day.

C. W. NEVILLE

So, having read what Mr. Neville thought of Peacehaven what do you think of it? I liked it, and naturally I stayed!

The many photographs and documents I have collected tell a story covering the history of Peacehaven and its early pioneers, who made that history possible. I hope you enjoy reading and studying the book, and if you, the reader, can offer any interesting items I shall be pleased to see them and pass them on to the County Archivist for posterity.

1. Peacehaven, c.1914. A typical view from the Dew Pond showing the arable lowlands in the distance and sheep grazing on the Downs.

2. Piddinghoe parish and the Downs, in 1914, as C. W. Neville must have seen it, before buying the land.

3. Lustrells Cottages, alas now demolished, were synonymous with the highly respected Rottingdean Copper family and especially 'Brasser' Copper, born here in 1810. Bob Copper the well-known television personality, author and broadcaster, continues the family name.

4. Shepherd's Cot, Stanley Road, in 1920, was approximately 9ft. x 6ft. x 6ft. to the eaves, with a chimney 8 ft. high. In the past the South Downs were farmed as sheep country. This required large flocks to be kept on the move by shepherds. During lambing season, usually a wet and cold period, the men would stay with the flocks day and night, and this cot is where the men would shelter during storms. It had a dirt floor and an open brick-built fireplace suitable to take chopped gorse wood. The door at the other end is much lower than doors in use today – indicating that in the past men were shorter. There were sheepfolds all around and also dewponds to water the sheep.

5. The tollgate and cottage, situated at Eastern Pylons on the A259. Tolls were paid here until 30 November 1881. The cottage was last occupied by Fred Wilton but the house was demolished in 1936 to facilitate road widening.

6. Two 18th-century cottages were in Peacehaven when C. W. Neville arrived. One was at Upper Hoddern, the other at Lower Hoddern. This cottage was situated at Upper Hoddern, and is now the site of the Youth Centre. Lower Hoddern was situated in the centre of a field, north of Bolney Avenue, but all the cottages were demolished in 1940.

7. The main road, then known as Dover Road, at Telscombe Cliffs in 1904. The photograph was taken looking east and shows the Portobello coastguards' station, on the right of the picture, and the cottages on the left. The cottages were built in 1791 and sold in 1891. The tall building in the distance was the post and telegraph office.

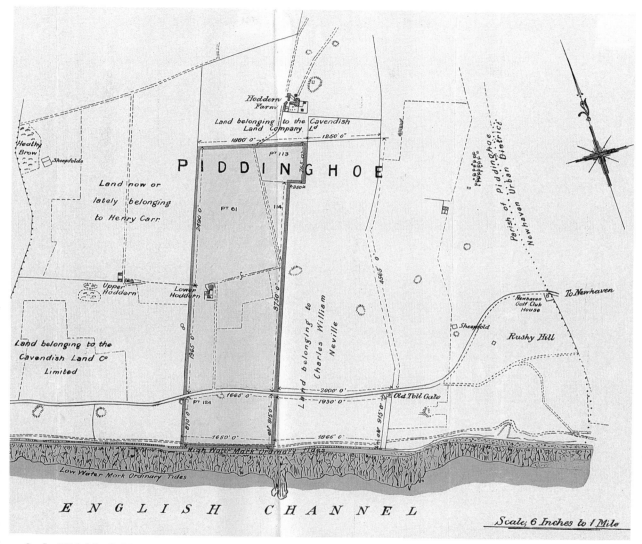

8. In 1914, Mr. C. W. Neville bought land at Piddinghoe, now part of Peacehaven, for £16,200 freehold. This picture of Telscombe Cliffs in 1904 shows the west side of Central Avenue and the original site of the post and telegraph office. Note the two circular pits on the south side of the main road, the larger one is now in the Dell. Today the Meridian Centre is positioned roughly at Upper Hoddern (*see* PT 61 on the map).

TELSCOMBE CLIFFS

Marine Operations (Aeroplane) Station.

(a) No. 514 Flight (D.H.6) of No. 242 Squadron. (b) 6th Brigade Landing Ground.
(S.W. Area; No. 10 (Operations) Group, 75th Wing.)

LOCATION.--England, Sussex, 3 miles west of Newhaven (pop., 6,300), 6 miles east of Brighton.

Railway Station:--Newhaven (L.B. & S.C. Rly.), $3\frac{1}{2}$ miles.

Road:--A new approach road from the main Brighton to Newhaven road.

FUNCTION.--(a) Station for No. 514 (D.H. 6) Flight of No. 242 Squadron (H.Q. at Newhaven), for Inshore Anti-submarine Patrol duties. This Squadron is under the control of the Commander-in-Chief, Portsmouth, for Operations.

(b) 6th Brigade Landing Ground (Day).

ESTABLISHMENT.

Personnel				Transport.			
Officers	..	..	.. 12	Light Tender	..	..	1
W.O.'s and N.C.O's above				Heavy Tenders	..	..	2
the rank of Corporal		.. 5		Motor Cycles ..	..	..	2
Rank and File	..	.. 30		Sidecar	..	..	1
				Trailers	..	..	2
TOTAL	..	..	.. 47	TOTAL	..	..	8

Machines.--D.H. 6 6

AERODROME.--Maximum dimensions in yards, 550 X 500. Area, 50 acres. Height above sea level, 120 feet. Soil, partly clay, partly sandy loam. Surface, moderate, portions are good, mostly very undulating. Slope towards the sea to the south, a depression in the middle. General surroundings : open, undulating down country with large fields, village close by to the west. The sea, with high cliffs, is immediately to the south.

TENURE POLICY.--Not on the list of permanent stations.

ACCOMMODATION.--2 Aeroplane Sheds--each 120' X 60'. Personnel is in Armstrong huts or billeted. There is a small Camp Guard hut which also serves as dining room.

9. During the First World War a government agent was sent to Peacehaven to requisition land for the building of an aerodrome and a Ministry of Agriculture farm at Chatsworth Park on what is now the school site. Three units of No. 78 Squadron – formed at Harrietsham on 1 November 1916 as a home defence unit – were based here until the squadron was disbanded in December 1919. The buildings were then converted to a rehabilitation centre for wounded ex-officers who wished to take up poultry farming but this lasted only a few years before most of the buildings were either demolished or removed. Only two buildings remained and became private residences until the 1950s, before they too were finally demolished and replaced by new housing.

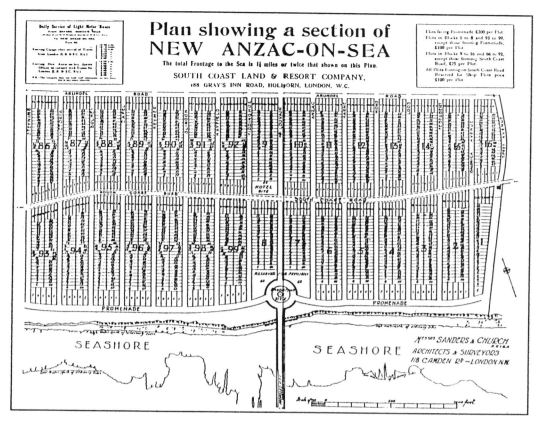

10. A 1916 grid plan showing the layout of the plots of land of 'New Anzac-on-Sea'.

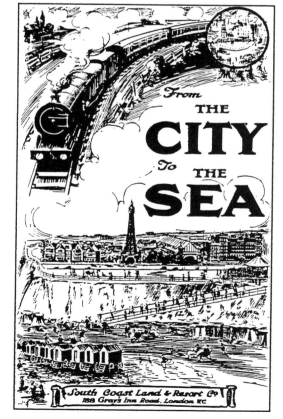

11. A 1916 advertisement showing an imaginary view of the estate that Mr. Neville originally dubbed 'The city to the sea'. It was later renamed New Anzac-on-Sea, but after the butchery at the Dardanelles the name was considered inappropriate and in 1917 the name of Peacehaven was finally settled upon. Note the beach steps, tower, pier, bandstand and pavilion, innovations which unfortunately were never developed.

A Seaside Home for £350

HAVE YOUR OWN SEASIDE HOME

On the South Coast — It will pay for itself

£50 down, the balance as rent to approved purchasers, on the

BEACH ESTATE, TELSCOMBE

Facing the Open Sea.   Close to Brighton, with ten-minute 'bus service.

. . *Live on the glorious South Downs for* . .
HEALTH AND HAPPINESS
Every site commands views over Sea and Downs

For full particulars apply to

**THE SECRETARY, PEACEHAVEN ESTATES, LTD.
PEACEHAVEN, SUSSEX**

12. 'A Seaside Home for £350', was the banner headline for this advertisement, *c.*1929. I wonder how much the bungalow in the picture, with such an uninterrupted sea view, and tennis courts virtually on the doorstep, would cost today?

13. In 1917 two name boards were prominently displayed, on the South Coast Road (A259), at each end of The Estate. Originally bearing the name of New Anzac-on-Sea they were later changed to Peacehaven. The Pylons, then known as Monoliths, were 20ft. high, but today only three remain.

14. The Peacehaven Estate Office was the first building erected in Peacehaven. It was used by Mr. Neville as a temporary home and office before it became a social centre for several years. It finally became a dairy, public tearoom and garden known as Rosemary and run by Mr. and Mrs. Thornton. Whist drives and dances, socials and lectures, societies and associations, all came into being at 'Thornton's'.

PEACEHAVEN:
Estate Office.

THE SOUTH COAST LAND & RESORT CO.

4 Vernon Place
London

Southampton Row
W.C.

March 3rd, 1917.

A. E. Harley, Esq.,
"Holmleigh",
Albany Rd,
Coventry.

Dear Sir,

We are in receipt of your remittance for
which you will find a formal receipt herewith.

The Deeds of Conveyance will be at once
placed in hand, and will on completion be forwarded
to Somerset House. Just as soon as the Deed is returned to us by the Authorities, we will forward it
to you by registered post.

The Deed of Conveyance contains a plan
showing the exact position of your plot.

Yours faithfully,
SOUTH COAST LAND & RESORT COMPANY.

Secretary.

**Please note that the name of
our South Coast Resort has been
changed as from February 12th
from New Anzac-on-Sea to**

PEACEHAVEN.

15. A letter of 3 March 1917 to a prospective buyer from the South Coast Land & Resort Company owned by Mr. Neville. At this point the name of The Estate was changed to Peacehaven.

16. In 1922, in order to promote Peacehaven, the estate company laid on a special Pullman train from Victoria to Brighton. Known as the Peacehaven Express, it transported members of the press, notables and the general public. A food and drinks party was organised in a marquee near the *Peacehaven Hotel*, and a British gliding exhibition was held by Fokker, all sponsored by the company.

17. Inside the marquee at lunch time, prior to a conducted tour of the estate. In a speech Mr. Neville gave for the occasion, and reported in *The Peacehaven Post* of 1 November 1922, he said that 'Peacehaven extended from close to the boundary of Newhaven almost to Rottingdean, and comprised nearly 2,500 acres; with some 300 homes, and applications for building licences increasing every day'.

PEACEHAVEN

ON THE GLORIOUS SOUTH DOWNS FACING THE OPEN SEA

Come to the Sunny South Coast
for
HEALTH *and* HAPPINESS

18.   An estate brochure given to prospective buyers in 1917. The marble statue, which was positioned in the hall of the *Peacehaven Hotel*, depicted 'Peace'. It was sculpted by Professor Vechi, of the University of Florence.

FREE GIFT OF A £1,125 HOUSE & LAND ! !

PEACEHAVEN

THE SOUTH COAST RESORT ALMOST FIVE MILES IN LENGTH FACING THE SEA

The Directors of Peacehaven Estates Ltd., are again making a great offer to those who purchase Freehold Land in the Peacehaven Estates between Nov. 1st, 1925, and Oct. 31st, 1926, namely: The Free Gift of a £1,125 Freehold House and Land on which it stands. This Offer is Open to All.

FROM a Garden City by the Sea Peacehaven is rapidly becoming a Seaside Resort of the first magnitude. It is almost five miles in length, facing the sea, and is acknowledged to be the greatest Seaside town planning and land development enterprise yet undertaken in this country. In a little over four years Peacehaven has grown from a hamlet of 24 residents to a busy, thriving sea coast resort, comprising approximately 4,000 people. There is no doubt that the ideal situation of Peacehaven, in the heart of Downland, within a short bus ride from Brighton, and just over an hour's journey from London, together with its wonderful, invigorating, health-promoting air, and rich, fertile soil, have contributed to its unique success.

HOW TO SECURE THE £1,125 FREEHOLD HOUSE AND LAND, FREE.

The Presentation House can be seen by visitors to Peacehaven at any time, and is ideally situated on one of the choicest sections of the Peacehaven Estates.

It is a two-storey building, containing large living room, three bedrooms, bathroom, kitchen, larder, and other domestic accommodations. It is a real labour-saving home, water laid on, ready for immediate occupation, and is immensely admired by all who have seen it.

Magnificent views of Downland and the English Channel can be obtained from its windows. Within a few hundred yards there is a frequent service of buses passing on the Brighton Road. By bus Brighton is only a 25 minutes' journey, while Newhaven Town is only 10 minutes away.

THE SIMPLE CONDITIONS

relating to this Presentation house and Land are as follows :—
(1) **Plots of land are offered for sale from 1st November, 1925, to 31st October, 1926,** as set out in the Application Form.
(2) **A list of all the purchasers of plots mentioned in Condition 1 will be made and such list of purchasers will be closed on 31st October, 1926.**
(3) **On the 10th November, 1926, a complimentary Luncheon** will be given by Peacehaven Estates Ltd., to which every such purchaser who has complied with the terms of his purchase will be invited by due notice to attend.
(4) **Immediately after the Luncheon, the purchasers will hold a meeting among themselves (a) to determine by a majority the method by which it shall be decided to whom the presentation House and Land shall be given ; (b) to carry out such decision.**
(5) **Upon such decision being announced and made known to Peacehaven Estates Ltd., the Company will forthwith convey the above mentioned Presentation House and Land to the chosen purchaser.**
(6) **No one employed by Peacehaven Estates Ltd., either at Peacehaven or at their London Offices in any capacity whatsoever will be permitted to avail themselves of this Offer.**

The above terms and conditions of this Offer will be rigidly and regularly complied with.

OUR FREE OFFER FULLY EXPLAINED.

To take advantage of our Free Offer all you have to do is to forward the attached application form, together with the sum of One Pound, as a first payment towards the cost of a Freehold Plot on the Peacehaven Estates, the most healthy, most bracing, and most rapidly rising Seaside Resort in the British Isles. The balance can be paid by convenient monthly cash instalments if desired. Everybody ought to own a bit of England, and the fact that Freehold Land at Peacehaven has in many cases trebled and quadrupled in value within the past three or four years, and is continuing to eclipse all previous records, makes the investment well worth serious consideration. No better or safer investment can possibly be made than buying Freehold Land in a rapidly rising and progressive community. There is something sound and substantial about it; it is always there, and in a growing town cannot depreciate. Once in your family it passes from father to son, and gradually becomes your most precious possession. The promoters of Peacehaven are striving and doing their level best to make Peacehaven the ideal Seaside Resort on the South Coast, and their plans are being rapidly realised.

THE ATTRACTIONS OF PEACEHAVEN.

A permanent way at a cost of several thousands of pounds has been made from the cliff to the foreshore, so that children and others can easily and quickly get to the sea for bathing and the joys of rock-pools and beach. In its corporate and civic life Peacehaven possesses an abounding vitality. It has many shops and tea gardens, and Hotel Peacehaven, for its size, is the most beautiful, convenient and up-to-date on the South Coast. Peacehaven has four churches, a College and school, a splendid dance hall, and a theatre and cinema. There are tennis courts, an excellent golf course, bowling greens and a cricket field, an open space of almost 200 acres, a park of 18 acres, and several smaller recreation grounds. There are a flourishing Literary and Debating Society, a Philharmonic and Dramatic Society, Tennis Clubs, Bowling Club, &c., &c. There is a local newspaper and a monthly magazine, "The Downland Post and Sussex Magazine," a copy of which will be sent post free on request, together with other particulars of Peacehaven by you sending a post card to the Secretary, Peacehaven Estates Ltd., Dept. L., Peacehaven, Sussex.

HOW TO GET THERE.

You can get to Peacehaven by train from London Bridge or Victoria to Brighton or Newhaven Town Station, and there is a frequent bus service from the Aquarium, Brighton, or from Newhaven. Our motor conveyance meets at Brighton Station the trains leaving Victoria daily at 9.5 a.m., 10.5 a.m. and 11.5 a.m., also 12.5 p.m. on Saturdays only. Our visitors are taken direct to Peacehaven without charge, where our representatives will welcome you and place every facility at your disposal to assist you with your investigations.

WHAT YOU MUST DO TO-DAY.

Fill in the application form to-day and make a profitable investment. There is a limit to the Freehold building sites we have available at Peacehaven, and they are being taken up quickly. Take advantage of our Free Gift Offer to-day and on receipt of the form duly filled in a copy of our new illustrated 80-page book with full particulars of Peacehaven will be sent you post free.

FILL IN THIS FORM & FORWARD TO-DAY.

To the Secretary,

THE PEACEHAVEN ESTATES, Ltd. Peacehaven, Sussex.

Herewith I forward the sum of £1, which please place to my credit as a first payment towards the cost of a £50 site of Freehold land on the Peacehaven Estates. The site shall contain not less than 2,500 square feet. Please select the best available site of this value which, subject to approval on inspection, I agree to purchase. If convenient to me I undertake to inspect within two months and reserve the right to change the site for any other available, of the same value, that I may prefer at the time of inspection. I also reserve the right to pay the balance in monthly instalments of £1 each, or by cash within 60 days at a discount of 5 per cent.

Name...

Address..

Occupation.................... Date................

Every purchaser of a Freehold Site of Land on the Peacehaven Estates between November 1st, 1925, and October 31st, 1926, will be put on the list of purchasers in respect of the £1,125 Presentation House and Land. A copy of our new 80-page booklet illustrating the life and history of Peacehaven will be forwarded to each purchaser.

POST THIS APPLICATION FORM to Peacehaven Estates, Ltd., Dept. L., Peacehaven, Sussex.

London Address :
Peacehaven House, 7, Pall Mall East, S.W.1 (near Trafalgar Square).

19. A brochure advertising freehold land on the Peacehaven Estates in 1925-26. By way of incentive the advertisements offered a free gift in the form of a house but on condition the buyer bought a plot of land.

Free Gift of a £1125 House

Together with the Freehold Site on which it stands

Entirely new Freehold Homes, Company Water, Electric Light, modern conveniences, from £500 to £2,000 each.

Magnificent large sites, ready for immediate building from £50 each.

Every purchaser of a Freehold Site on the Peacehaven Estates up till October 31st, 1926, is entitled to participate in our

FREE GIFT OFFER OF A £1,125 FREEHOLD HOUSE

together with the site upon which it stands.

CASH COUPON VALUE £5.

To the Secretary,

THE PEACEHAVEN ESTATES, LIMITED, Peacehaven, Sussex.

Herewith I forward this coupon value £5 (Five Pounds) which please place to my credit as a first payment towards the cost of a £50 site of Freehold land on the Peacehaven Estates. The site shall contain not less than 2,500 square feet. Please select the best available site of this value which, subject to approval on inspection, I agree to purchase. If convenient to me I undertake to inspect within two months and reserve the right to change the site for any other available, of the same value, that I may prefer at the time of inspection. I also reserve the right to pay the balance in monthly instalments of £1 each, or by cash within 60 days at a discount of 5 per cent.

Every purchaser of a Freehold Site of Land on the Peacehaven Estates between November 1st, 1925, and October 31st, 1926, will be put on the list of purchasers in respect of the £1,125 Presentation House.

A certificate entitling you to participate will be sent in due course.

Name ....

Address ....

Occupation ....

POST THIS COUPON to the Peacehaven Estates, Limited, Peacehaven, Sussex.

London Address: Peacehaven House, 7, Pall Mall East, S.W.1 (near Trafalgar Square).

SPECIAL GIFTS TO SUBSCRIBERS TO THE "DOWNLAND POST."

A choice Freehold Site on the Peacehaven Estates, value

£100

will be given to the Annual Subscriber who introduces the largest number of new annual subscribers to our magazine up to and inclusive of 30th June, 1926.

In addition a Free Coupon Value

£10

towards the purchase of a £50 Freehold Site will be awarded to every Annual Subscriber who introduces fifty or more new annual subscribers up to and inclusive of 30th June, 1926.

For this purpose a special form on which will appear the names both of the new subscriber and of the introducer is being issued.

The Editor of the "Downland Post" will be pleased to send you as many forms as you can use, if you will be so good as to forward the attached requisition.

REQUISITION FORM.

To the Editor

The "DOWNLAND POST"

Peacehaven, Sussex.

Dear Sir,

Please send me .... (fill in the number of copies required) copies of the Special Subscription Form to the *Downland Post*, which I propose to use for the purpose of obtaining new annual subscribers to your magazine at the advertised rate of Five Shillings per annum to run from the date of the subscription form.

It is understood that this application is entirely free and carries no obligation whatever.

Yours faithfully,

(Name) ....

(Address) ....

....

20, 21 & 22. A similar advertising venture was started by the *Downland Post*, but with added prizes for its own subscribers. One hundred pounds was being offered to the subscriber who introduced the largest number of new annual subscribers to the paper and £10 to the subscriber who introduced fifty of more new annual subscribers. The eventual winner of the presentation house (bottom, right) was Miss A. T. Jackson who had established the Norwood and Norbury College of Music.

23 & 24.   Small wood and asbestos buildings were first built in Peacehaven, in 1920. Six buildings were initially built just off the South Coast Road in Seaview Avenue. Today, only one remains on the east side of the avenue. These buildings like many in the village were constructed from secondhand war surplus huts purchased from Seaford army camp. New, flat asbestos sheets were used to cover the framework of 4 ins. x 2 ins. timber, and the roof covered with diagonal flat asbestos tiles. The price of the freehold varied from between £325 to £450. Waste was disposed of either directly into a cesspit or with the aid of buckets! There were no other public services.

   After the First World War building materials were in very short supply and with the country virtually bankrupt little money was available for construction. Secondhand materials had to be used, such as cheap asbestos from Spain and bricks either produced locally at the Brickie or imported from Belgium. Illustration 24 shows the first masonry building constructed in Peacehaven, in 1923.

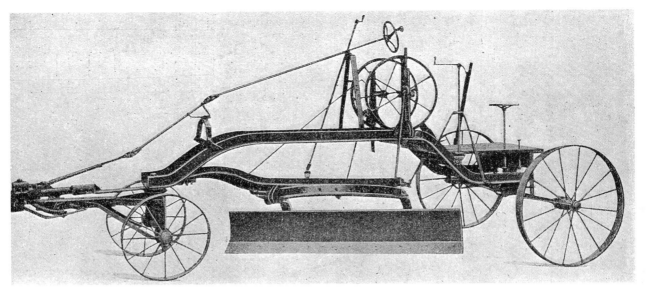

25. In the early 1920s the Sawyer-Massey tractor was used for grading the soil for the proposed avenues and roads of The Estate. A 40-mile stretch of roadway was graded but once it had been graded the grass was allowed to grow back again and only painted avenue signs indicated where you were.

26. The *Lord Hartington*, seen here in 1923, was a small coaster that ferried bricks from Belgium to Newhaven.

27. The Brickie and its workers – note how young some of them were! With little in the way of landmarks, it is difficult to know where on the estate the brick works was situated. However, if you look just behind the horse, in the middle distance, Roderick Avenue is just visible.

28. The Peacehaven Estate Company's yard in 1922. The vehicle shed, joinery works and mechanical stores were being constructed with all the most modern machinery in order to accelerate construction and lessen the cost of building.

29. A cartoon drawn by Gordon Volk for *The Peacehaven Post* in March 1922. The caption describes the race to build at Peacehaven as 'having assumed the nature of a sporting event', under the heading, 'The Race for the 'Home' Stakes'.

30 & 31. Peacehaven Estate Company's yard in 1922 was located on the South Coast Road to the Promenade – Piddinghoe to Sunview Avenues. It housed, amongst other things, garages, workshops, offices, blacksmith's shop, stables and housing for the site workers. It manufactured such things as doors, window-frames and all the paraphernalia that could be factory produced, and relieved the unemployment of adjacent areas by employing large numbers of plumbers, electricians, carpenters and painters etc.

32. Peacehaven Engineering Works and Wood-working Plant in the 1920s.

33 & 34.   In the 1920s unemployment was very high and large numbers of men converged on Peacehaven hoping to find work of one sort or another. The Estate Company employed up to 1,000 men, affectionately nicknamed the 'Concrete Busy Bees' by Mr. Neville due to their hard work. They operated various forms of transport such as horses and carts, steam lorries and steamrollers. The company office, seen here in 1921, was used for selling building materials. It was situated on the main road at the north-east corner of Piddinghoe Avenue, and bears an uncanny resemblance to a scene from the wild west.

35. This 1924 charabanc provided a useful service between Peacehaven and adjacent towns, and was much in demand by football enthusiasts and dancing parties at Lureland Hall.

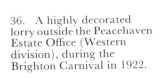

36. A highly decorated lorry outside the Peacehaven Estate Office (Western division), during the Brighton Carnival in 1922.

37. The *Downland Post*, a monthly publication that was circulated throughout Sussex, and the brainchild of Mr. Neville, was first published in 1921 and was originally called the *Peacehaven Post*.

38. Optima Stores was the first post office to open in Peacehaven. It was owned by Mr. A. E. Parker (seen here) on the site where the main post office is now situated. Note the advertisements for the locally produced Kerr's Peacehaven Toffees, and the *Peacehaven Post* – from where I gathered so much of the local history.

39. The West End Stores owned by J. Blewett in 1923, was situated on the corner of Lincoln Avenue and South Coast Road.
It has since been demolished (1980) and replaced by a block of flats.

40. In the summer of 1920 Mr. Neville employed hundreds of men to help lay out the Estate's roadways and paths and to clean up the neglected and pothole-ridden main road. The workmen worked very hard, and in the summer heat quickly developed a thirst. Unfortunately Peacehaven had no public house, so Mr. Neville organised the building of a large wooden shed, complete with wooden bar, on the corner of Keymer Avenue. It was eventually opened as an off-licence before being taken over by F. Burden (seen here with his son) and sold beer at 4d. a pint. Business was brisk and hundreds of pints of beer were sold each day.

41. Mr. A. E. Parker sold Optima Stores to open another shop called Arcadia, further along the road on the corner of Central Avenue, Telscombe Cliffs, 1923.

42. The first Peacehaven garage, built in February 1922, was opened by N. F. Edwards on the corner of Steyning Avenue and was made entirely of reinforced concrete, as bricks were hard to come by. It was demolished in 1965 and replaced by an engineering works.

43. The sub-post office and grocery store on Roderick Avenue, in the 1920s. Owned by Mr. and Mrs. Sayers – seen here outside the shop with a Ford Popular van which could be bought brand new for £100 – a fondly remembered couple who supplied the needs of the many unemployed during the 1930s.

44. Mr. J. H. Pillinger, seen here in 1926, opened his shop in 1924 at Steyning Avenue to sell cigarettes, sweets, minerals and teas. In c.1928 it became the *Dewdrop Inn* and over the years has been extended several times to become a firmly established and popular public house.

45. Barclays Bank first opened on the South Coast Road opposite the *Peacehaven Hotel* in the early 1920s. It was later moved to its present site on the corner of Roderick Avenue.

46. The second bank to be built in Peacehaven was the Midland Bank on the South Coast Road. It was erected by the Peacehaven Building and Supply Co. Ltd., in 1923, and served a population of 1,500 people. It continued to operate until 1939 but was forced to close due to the outbreak of the Second World War. It now operates as a take-away.

47. The confectionery and tobacconist's shop of Mr. G. E. Buck in 1923. Situated on the corner of Victoria Avenue, it was an early established business in Peacehaven and owned by Mr. Buck for 10 years until it was purchased by Mr. F. A. King, c.1933. The lamp post outside the shop was bought by Mr. King who provided it with electricity from the shop's supply, whilst a petrol pump outside the shop, delivered a measure of petrol to refill a cigarette lighter when an old halfpenny was inserted. Today it is an ironmonger's shop, owned by the author's family, and has remained virtually unchanged, despite the severe storm in 1987 which caused £100,000 worth of damage.

48. The greengrocer's shop owned by the author's father during the 1930s, seen here on the occasion of the summer village carnival in the mid-1930s.

49. Mr. A. E. Mansfield's butcher's shop on the corner of Sunview Avenue and South Coast Road in 1922. Mr. Mansfield began his career as a Newhaven barrow boy selling meat from a stall. His son, sitting on the doorstep, is still around today.

50. The premises of Mr. W. Kenney were sub-let to various traders and included a café and restaurant, seen here in 1924. When the buildings were being constructed, the foreman often caught his workmen drinking tea instead of working. One night, unbeknown to the men, he installed a china teapot on the ridge of the roof, which is still there today. The building later became a bridge club, before becoming a public house called the *Gay Highlander* and then the *Sussex Trader*.

51. The premises, seen here in 1923 and situated on the corner of Edith Avenue, was originally a restaurant and bakery owned by the Shepherd family. It was taken over in the early '20s by Mr. and Mrs. H. Barker as a café and restaurant. The Barkers, having just returned from Kenya, renamed the building, Kenya House, reminding us of the fact that many early inhabitants of the village were colonials returning to Great Britain after serving abroad. In 1929 the building was purchased by Mr. Deal who converted it to a social club called the Central Club which still continues today.

52. The cycle shop owned by Mr. Butt, early in the 1920s. A few years later it became a motorcycle shop before being taken over by Mr. Fenner who converted it to a garage. In 1970 it was taken over by Mr. Stowell and is still operating as a garage.

53. Mr. W. A. Wood, standing outside the café entrance of his garage, on the corner of Vernon Avenue in 1924. His son can be seen on the right-hand side, by the garage doors.

54. Mr. L. Woods, the author's uncle, seen standing in the doorway of his butcher's shop in 1922. It was situated on the corner of Southdown Avenue, the first butcher's shop to be built in Peacehaven. Note the early American van with its steering wheel on the left-hand side and the spare wheel – a tyre on a rim. Silhouetted against the windows of Mr. Woods' shop can be seen the outline of Stan Butt's shop opposite.

55. Mr. Winkworth's General Hardware Stores on the corner of the main road and Horsham Avenue. It was converted to a dentist's surgery in the early 1960s and continues this function today.

56. The Rosemary Tea Rooms and Dairy on the South Coast Road (*see* illustration 14).

57. The Rosemary Tea Gardens on the corner of Piddinghoe Avenue, in 1921. Seen here with Mr. Neville are the staff and some of the pioneer traders, including Mr. Lew Wood, the butcher and his wife Mrs. Amy Wood, Mr. Frank Thornton, butcher's manager, and the post-master and owner of the post office.

58. Looking west towards Rosemary Tea Gardens, *c*.1925.

59.   Looking west from Wellington Road in 1950.

60.   Looking east from Barclays Bank in the late 1920s.

61. South Coast Road looking west with the post office and Slindon Avenue on the right, in the late 1950s.

62. The *Castle Hotel* on the left, looking west in the late 1930s. It became fully licensed about 20 years ago and, although no longer residential, is still operating as a public house known as *The Retreat*.

63.   Looking east from Keymer Avenue. The first building on the left is the post office which was the first shop to be built in Peacehaven. The building in the right foreground is now operating as Giles, plumber. (Note the telegraph poles which carried telephone wires between Newhaven and Brighton.)

64.   Phyllis Avenue seen from the south side of the main road in 1922. Behind the estate office board is the new Barclays Bank which was soon to be opened on two half days a week!

65.   Mr. Frank Hickford owned and ran this small general store in Roderick Avenue for 40 years. It was constructed in 1924 based on the design of the army huts. The elevated water tank in the distance served the houses in this area. The store was demolished in 1992.

66.   Looking north up Roderick Avenue at Firle Road, in 1956. In the early 1920s the shop on the right was known as Hutchings Bakeries and it continued as a bakery until 1952. Note how peaceful the scene once was.

67.   South Coast Road in 1925 with the first Peacehaven Petrol Station on the left. On the right is a well advertised wall sign, 'Plots of land £20 Freehold'. This site is at the junction of Steyning Avenue. Note how muddy and rutted the roads are.

68. The Rosemary Tea Rooms, South Coast Road, 1925. Note the roughly made road with little more than a path to act as pavement. All that protected the pedestrian from the car were lumps of concrete.

Hotel Peacehaven

Grand Opening, Friday, September 29, 1922

GALA DAY, SPORTS, FIREWORKS AND SUPER BEACON FIRES

The date has now been fixed for the opening of Peacehaven's beautiful Hotel Palace, and arrangements are being made to ensure the occasion being an impressive and memorable one. It will be a brilliant ensemble to celebrate the close of Peacehaven's successful and highly prosperous second Summer Season.

SPECIAL PULLMAN CARS

will be reserved to convey, from all parts of the country, distinguished guests and visitors, who will be entertained at a **Grand Luncheon Banquet.**

The guests will be conducted in special cars on a tour of inspection through the **developments of Peacehaven.**

A first class

MILITARY BAND

will play in the sunken Italia Gardens, and an Orchestra in the Hotel Lounge.

There will be

SPORTS AND PASTIMES

arranged for the entertainment of vistors and residents, including a **Baby Show**, with substantial prizes for the bonniest Peacehaven babies, and **Beauty Competition**, with similar recognition for the prettiest ''babies'' of the Garden City. Photographs of the winners will appear exclusively in the London Press.

At dusk the proceedings will be crowned by a **Grand Finale** of

WONDERFUL FIREWORKS

arranged and operated by **Brock & Co.,** of **Crystal Palace Fame.** The programme of illuminations will include: Aerial Maroons, Prismatic ''Fairyland,'' Magical Aurora Borealis and African Moonlight with Shower of Emeralds, Rainbow Cloud, Showers of Violets, Golden and Silver Scroll and Shimmering Streamers. Also combinations comprising Clusters of Stars, Canopy of Jewels, Hissing Snakes, The Golden Gnome, Firework Jugglery, Verdant Fireflies, Alladin's Tree, Lattice of Pearls, Burma Rubies, Jasmine Sprays, Venetian Flower Baskets, Giant Ospreys, ''Pentapyric'' Shells, Northern Star Parachute, Fairy Flower Ropes, Opalescent Fountains, Alpine Lightballs, Fiery Nightbirds, Niagara Falls by Moonlight, ''The Mystery of the East,'' ''The Pilot of the Night,'' ''The Whirlwind,'' ''The Gymnastic Monkey,'' ''The Orb of Empire,'' ''Thunderbolt Bombardment,'' and **"Goodnight."**

A COLOSSAL BONFIRE

will be ignited, which will be seen not only throughout the Downlands, but, if the night is clear, from the **Shores of France.**

Friday, September 29, 1922

LONG LIVE QUEEN PEACEHAVEN!

69. An advertisement for the grand opening of the *Hotel Peacehaven* on Friday, 29 September 1922.

70 & 71.   The artist, Gordon Volk, son of Magnus Volk, of Brighton electric railway fame, was employed by Mr. Neville to draw the proposed designs for the *Peacehaven Hotel* and sunken Italian gardens.

72. *Peacehaven Hotel* was built in 1922 and cost £10,000 to build and £5,000 to furnish. It was a showpiece of elegance with marble floors, oak pannelling and each bedroom was complete with hot and cold running water. It housed bowling greens, tennis courts, landscape gardens and a greenhouse. In 1987 the hotel was demolished under the long serving and popular landlord Roger Lythgoe.

73. This public house adjoined the *Peacehaven Hotel* and was known as the *Shades*. It fronted on to the South Coast Road, but has long since been demolished and the site is now a car-park.

74. This picture shows the same location as illustration 73, but after the demolition of the *Shades*.

75. The *Peacehaven Hotel* garages and the Peacehaven charabanc in 1923.

76. The entrance to Lureland Hall in 1923. The hall was for many years the only social hall of any size in the area. It is still in existence as a social club.

77. Inside Lureland Hall in 1923. Dancing was held here every weekend with music being provided by a resident three-piece band. The sprung floor was specially built and was widely publicised.

78 & 79. The *Peacehaven Hotel* was a popular place for social gatherings. The grounds of the hotel were always available for functions, such as maypole dancing, leisure activities and charity events. It was managed by Roger L. Lythgoe for fifteen years up to the time of its demolition in 1987.

80. The hotel and grounds were purchased by the Kemp Town Brewery Brighton Ltd. for £8,500 on 19 September 1939.

81 & 82.   The three-hundred seat Pavilion was constructed by the Estate Company in 1923. It was erected on the south side of the main road at Sutton Avenue and was originally a theatre. It hosted a variety of entertainments including boxing, plays and pantomime. The Peacehaven Operatic Society performed Gilbert and Sullivan operas here, often conducted by Mr. Felix Powell, composer of 'Pack up your troubles in your old kit bag'.

83 & 84. After the Pavilion Theatre became a cinema, *c*.1929, it was soon able to boast of talkie films before they were presented at Newhaven. In this 1930 hoarding advertising the main features, seat prices ranged between 6d., 9d. and 1s.

SEPTEMBER, 1925.

PICTURELAND

Issued by

PAVILION THEATRE,
PEACEHAVEN.

UNDER NEW MANAGEMENT

First-Class Pictures and Star Varieties.

CONTINUOUS PERFORMANCES from 6 to 10 p.m.

MATINEES : Wednesdays and Saturdays, 2.30 p.m.

PAVILION CINEMA
PEACEHAVEN

NIGHTLY AT 6 p.m.   CONTINUOUS.   DOORS OPEN 5.45 p.m.

MONDAY, TUESDAY & WEDNESDAY, MAY 9th, 10th & 11th.

JOHNNY WEISSMULLER & MAUREEN O'SULLIVAN in

TARZAN ESCAPES

Also PERCY MARMONT and LOUIS GOODRICH in

THE CAPTAIN'S TABLE

THURSDAY, FRIDAY & SATURDAY, MAY 12th, 13th & 14th.

OLIVIA DE HAVILLAND, IAN HUNTER & ROLAND YOUNG in

CALL IT A DAY

Also DICK FORAN in

LAND BEYOND THE LAW

PRICES: **6**D., **9**D. **& 1/-** (INCLUDING TAX).

CHILDREN 3d. & 6d.

85. In February 1940 the 17-year-old Pavilion was burnt to the ground when a fire started in the projection room shortly after the commencement of the first performance. The blaze was said to have lit up the sky for miles around and within three hours from the time of the outbreak the building was completely gutted, despite the best attempts to put it out by Chief Officer W. B. Powell and the Newhaven Auxiliary Fire Service, under Chief Officer S. Gray.

86. Peacehaven Fire Brigade, seen here in 1938, were based at Fenner's Garage (now Stowell's Garage). The Bedford fire engine – with a 30-cwt chassis fitted with towing trailer and mounted water pump was owned originally by Chailey Rural District Council but was taken over by the National Fire Brigade before the Second World War. The crew include; Chief Officer Powell, Driver Ray Fenner; Firemen: Bert Stubberfield, Harold Wagstaff, Stan Price, Don Radcliffe, Jack Jefferies, Arthur Blake, Ted Blake, Tom Caffyn, Frank Bailey, and Fred Bailey.

87 & 88.   Resident agents outside the Estate Office and the same building but now known as Rosemary Café and Gardens. For several years the office was C. W. Neville's home and workshop. With few modern conveniences, he obtained drinking water from the well at the tollgate which was demolished in 1936.

89 & 90.   The Eastern Estate Office at the corner of Mayfield Avenue in 1922. It was the third business opened by Neville to cope with the demand for properties. The Model T-Ford seen outside the office was used to patrol the estate by the company's policemen, Mr. Davies and Mr. Parker, seen standing to attention in uniform. Although they had no police powers they kept an eye on the Estate.

91.   The second Eastern Estate Offices were built in 1922, across the road from the first office, to cope with the demand. They employed a staff of about twenty.

92.   The new estate offices of the South Coast Land & Resort Co. Ltd., in 1924. They were built by the Peacehaven Building & Supply Company Ltd., opposite the *Peacehaven Hotel*, on South Coast Road. In the doorway are (*left to right*) Mr. Felix Powell, Mrs. Sangster and Mr. Wallace Sangster – Agents and Chief Agent respectively.

93.   The Western Estate Office, seen here in 1925, was situated on the corner of Central Avenue and the South Coast Road, at Telscombe Cliffs. Between 1900-20 the estate office building was originally the Post and Telegraph Office. The chauffeur-driven car, was owned by Mr. Neville, and transported potential customers around the estate to choose their plots of land. For many people the car ride alone was quite a thrill, as often it was the first time they had been in a car.

94.   In 1924 an emergency tent was erected opposite the Western Estate Office, on the South Coast Road. It was a temporary office set up to cope with the enormous influx of land buyers.

95.   The estate office at Rottingdean on the South Coast Road, situated between Little Crescent and Chailey Avenue, in 1923.

96.   A corrugated-iron construction was temporarily erected by the council in 1924, at Cliff Park, as a school. Known as the 'Old Tin' school, it was presided over by the headmaster Mr. Blackman and catered for about one hundred children. Mr. Sam Smith (seen fifth from the right) and Mrs. Sam Smith (wearing the round glasses) were pupils of the school at this time. It operated as a school until the start of the Second World War when it was closed down and remained abandoned until it was demolished in 1951.

97.   A 'Victory in Europe' party held at Lureland Hall in 1945. On the left is Mr. Wilmshurst and opposite him the Rev. Martyn Harries. Behind Rev. Harries are Sid Mepsted and Mr. Woodruffe.

Band of the Royal Field Artillery

98. The band of the Royal Field Artillery in the mid-1920s. They were taking part in one of the many events organised by Charles W. Neville as a public relations exercise for Peacehaven.

99. Many horses were used during the early 1920s in the transportation of building materials for Peacehaven's road construction, during the early 1920s.

100.   The first Peacehaven football team, seen here after achieving four successive victories, in 1921. On the back row, (*left to right*): G. Sweet, F. G. A. Kiff, E. R. Bernthal (linesman), S. Nelson, L. Venus, H. Cole, A. F. Whitefield (Secretary and Treasurer), A. Massey, W. Betts (goal), H. Sanders (Vice-Captain), L. E. Evershed and W. Fulford (Chairman). Seated (*left to right*): Frank Thornton (Captain), W. Venus, L. Gurney, W. C. Turner and C. Davis.

101.   The dining room of the *Peacehaven Hotel*, 30 May 1924. The occasion is the first annual dinner party of the Peacehaven Football Club.

102. Peacehaven Football Club, 1947-48 Cup winners. The photograph includes Reg Durrant, Solly Gardner, Chris Tucknott, Alf Durrant, Harold King, Les Pooley, Tony Gosling, Ted Redshaw, Fred Morris, Sandy Watts, Fred Preston, Dick Gosling, Ron Wallis, Basil Cornford, Nobby Sulton, Taffy Davis, Laurie Hows, Wally Powell, Walter Durrant, Brian Brown, Des Wood, George Jarman, Mr. Pooley, the dog, Tony Bashford, Frank Clasen, Jock Thompson, Ron Bassett, Gordon Tucknott, John Burgess, Phil Wiltshire, Frank Sexton, and Clem Lucas, the landlord of the *Dewdrop Inn* (middle row, fourth from the left).

103. The Telscombe and Peacehaven Football Club fixtures book for 1935-36.

TELSCOMBE AND PEACEHAVEN FOOTBALL CLUB.
FIXTURES FOR SEASON 1935-36.

Date	Opponents.	Venue	Result	Date	Opponents.	Venue	Result
1935				Dec. 14	Falmer	Away	
Sept. 7				21	Lewes " C "	Home	
14	Powis Rovers	Home		25			
21	Denton Rovers	Home		26	Bevis Athletic		
28	Falmer	Home		28	East Side	Home	
Oct. 5				**1936**			
	Preliminary Jnr. Cup			Jan. 4	Denton	Away	
12	Hamsey	Home			Semi-Final Charity Cup		
19	Iford	Away		11	Hamsey	Away	
	1st Round Charity Cup			18			
26	Barcombe	Away			3rd Round Jnr. Cup		
Nov. 2	Invicta	Home		25	Lewes " C "	Away	
9				Feb. 1	Seaford II.	Away	
	1st Round Jnr. Cup			8	Seaford II.	Home	
16	Telscombe or Iford v. Invicta	Home		15	East Side	Away	
	2nd Round Charity Cup			22			
23	Green's	Away		29	Green's	Home	
30				Mar. 7	Barcombe	Home	
	2nd Round Jnr. Cup			14	Rice Sports	Away	
Dec. 7				21	Rice Sports	Home	
	3rd Round Charity Cup			28	Invicta	Away	

Peacehaven Bowling Club's Fixtures, 1929.

Captain: J. P. GOBLE.

Vice-Captain: C. S. RICHARDS.

Match Secretary: J. WHITTLE.

Asst. Secretary: W. H. WHITMILL.

Date	Opponents		Green	Result	For	Against
May 1 W.	Captain *v.* Vice-Captain	…				
4 S.	Newhaven Men's Social	…	Home			
11 S.						
15 W.	Kingsway (Hove)	…	Home			
18 S.	Seaford Recreation	…	Away			
25 S.	Newhaven Recreation	…	Home			
29 W.						
June 1 S.	Queen's Park (Brighton)	…	Away			
8 S.						
15 S.						
19 W.	Newhaven (Sheffield)	…	Away			
26 W	Ditchling	…	Home			
29 S.						
July 3 W	Burgess Hill	…	Away			
10 W.	Burgess Hill	…	Home			
13 S.	Seaford Recreation	…	Home			
20 S.						
27 S.	Queen's Park	…	Home			
31 W.	Ditchling (Flower Show)	…	Away			
Aug 3 S.	Hove Park (Flower Show)		Away			
10 S	Men's Social	…	Open			
17 S.	Newhaven Recreation	…	Away			
24 S.	Kingsway (Hove)	…	Away			
28 W.						
31 S.	Newhaven (Sheffield)	…	Home			

104 & 105. Peacehaven Bowling Club at their annual party, in 1950. It was originally started in 1924 when a number of enthusiasts met at the *Peacehaven Hotel* to play on the hotel's two greens. Within a year the club had grown to such numbers that it decided to become affiliated with the Sussex County Bowling Association.

Mr. W. B. Powell (*see* caption 86) sold to the club some land he owned at Friars Bay. A pavilion was built, which provided dances, drives and concerts for the members and their friends. In the picture above are the Bagnall, Jerron, Gillett, Hunter, Hannan, Noakes, Radcliffe, Davis, Mansfield, Dunning, Parsons, Buck, Facks, Stoten, Fox, Heading, Holgate and Chapman families. I apologise to those people I have unfortunately failed to identify.

106. After the First World War there was a great deal of poverty in the country, especially in South Wales. Many miners and their families came to Peacehaven looking for work, the Davies family being one. Mr. Davies got a job at Peacehaven as village security officer, whilst his wife, a nurse and midwife ministered to all. Many women in distress and with no funds, sought her service in the hope she would help; she always did, often without payment. She never turned anyone away.

107. Peacehaven Cricket Juniors, shown here in 1930, includes (fifth from left) Mervyn Davies who was killed during the Second World War.

108. The Sussex Motor Cycle Club and Light Car Club met annually under the presidency of Mr. Neville. Here they can be seen at a Gymkhana on the Peacehaven Football Ground, in 1923.

109. Cricket on the Downs in 1923.

110. Competitors at the Tennis Tournament on the *Peacehaven Hotel* court in 1923.

Peacehaven Social Circle

Peacehaven Horticultural and Poultry Society

A preliminary meeting was held at "Rosemary" on Wednesday evening, April 12th, to consider the advisability of forming the above, when, in spite of unfortunately wet weather, a good representative attendance was registered. It was proposed, seconded and unanimously resolved that the Peacehaven Horticultural and Poultry Society be formed, and that its aims and objects shall be:

1.   To organise some scheme for co-operative buying, distributing, transport, and marketing.

2.   To promote lectures, demonstrations, and discussions.

3.   To become affiliated with the Agricultural Organization Society.

4.   To establish an information bureau for mutual help, and for the information and guidance of beginners.

5.   To hold an Annual Flower and Vegetable Show.

PEACEHAVEN HORTICULTURAL AND POULTRY SOCIETY.

The First GENERAL MEETING
will be held at "Rosemary" on
Friday, May 12th, at 7 p.m.
AGENDA :
1. **Report of Preliminary Meeting.**
2. **Election of Officers.**
3. **Constitution of Society, and Rules.**
4. **Other business.**

The Chair will be taken by Mr. G. H. Powell, Editor of PEACEHAVEN POST

All residents (ladies included) are cordially invited to attend.

A committee was formed, consisting of Mr. W. Sankey, Mr. T. T. Bates, Mr. J. Egerton, Mrs. Phelps, and Mrs. Day, to make arrangements for, and convene, the first general meeting, and to draft rules for the constitution of the Society.

At this preliminary meeting much enthusiasm was displayed, there is every sign that the Society will become established upon a firm basis, and grow and flourish, as Peacehaven is doing. All Peacehaveners can help, both as workers and supporters. There is a great deal to be done, and willing co-operation is essential if we are to achieve the general desire to hold the First Peacehaven Flower Show at the end of the present Summer.

Residents should not fail to attend the first general meeting, as announced on this page. Everything has to have a beginning, and everything begun in Peacehaven makes history, and builds up the future for ourselves and those who will follow us. Make a note of MAY 12TH.

Social at "Rosemary"

The second Peacehaven Social Gathering was held in the "Rosemary" Tea Lounge on Wednesday, April 5th. There were as many residents present as the room would accommodate, and a very jolly evening passed all too quickly. Refreshments were daintily served by Mrs. Thornton and her spick-and-span maids, and Mr. Thornton busied himself making everyone comfortable and at home.

A musical programme of exceptional variety, interspersed with stories and recitations brought to light the pleasing fact the Peacehaven is, perhaps, more richly endowed with entertaining talent than many places very much older and larger. And *everybody was happy.* The next "Social" will take place on Wed., May 24th.

Peacehaven Citizens' Association

This Association is now established, and a considerable number of residents are enrolled as members. The preliminary meeting was held at "Rosemary" on Friday, April 7th, when general principles were discussed, and it was unanimously decided that the Peacehaven Citizens' Association be formed, and that its object shall be to promote the mutual interests of its members. The date of the first general meeting was fixed for Thursday, April 20th. On this date a full meeting took place, and the following officers were unanimously elected : Chairman, Mr. A. E. Parker; Vice-Chairman, Mr. M. Phelps ; Secretary, Mr. A. S. Edwards ; Treasurer, Mr. T. E. Thornton. Committee : Messrs. S. Searle, J. Blewett, A. Kerr, W. Sankey, and Mrs. Mitchell. It was decided that the subscription for the present be 2s. 6d. per quarter, and that membership be limited to householders and their families over 18 years of age. The next meeting will be held at the Secretary's Residence, "First Acres," Firle Road, Peacehaven, on Thursday, May 18th, at 7.30 p.m.

111.   A page from *The Peacehaven Post*, 1 May 1922, concerning the Peacehaven Horticultural and Poultry Society meeting and a social at 'Rosemary'.

112. Peacehaven parish church and church hall were opened in Bramber Avenue in the early 1920s. The site is now occupied by the parish church hall.

113. The Peacehaven Catholic church situated between Horsham and Edith Avenues in spring 1925. The resident priest at the time was Rev. Fr. Cecil Bruet.

114 & 115. The United Free (Interdenominational) Church, situated on the corner of Bramber Avenue and Arundel Road. An article in *The Peacehaven Post* of 1 December 1922 made the announcement that the Lord Bishop of the Diocese would be arriving in Peacehaven the following day to dedicate the new church building and parish room. The building had taken less than a month to build, and although not complete it was functional. Seen outside the church in 1925 are: Henry Wagstaff, Nellie Sanders, Mr. Sanders, Mr. Eydon, Mr. Burdon, Mr. Shipway, Mr. Powell, Mr. Killick, Mr. Oxborrow, Mr. Benjaman, Mr. Barnard, Miss Barnard, Master Oxborrow, Master Wagstaff, Master Hill, Master Cunnington, Captain Mungavin.

PEACEHAVEN
FREE CHURCH
(MAYFIELD AVENUE, PEACEHAVEN)
MAGAZINE.

No. 41. MAY, 1928. Price 2d.

PASTOR: REV. W. L. MOORHOUSE,

THURSTON VILLA, DOROTHY AVENUE.

Divine Service on **Sundays at 11.0** a.m. and 6.30 p.m.

Prayer Meeting at close of Evening Service.

Sunday School at 3 o'clock.

Christian Endeavour, **Monday 7.0.** Choir Practice, **Monday**, 8.0.

Church **Fellowship** Class, Wednesday, 7.0.

This Church is licensed for Marriages.

PREACHERS FOR THE MONTH:

May	6	Mr. W. J. CALLINGHAM, Newhaven (m. & e.)
,,	13	THE PASTOR. Communion, evening service.
,,	20	SUNDAY SCHOOL ANNIVERSARY,
,,	27	THE PASTOR.

116. The *Peacehaven Free Church* magazine, May 1928.

117. In 1922, Mr. Neville became aware that the *Daily Mail* was in the process of sponsoring the first English gliding flight. To promote Peacehaven he offered the pilot, Mr. Fokker, £1,000 to fly at Peacehaven first, The newspaper was furious at being usurped and never forgave him. They finally held their display two weeks later.

118. The Gliding Exhibition, Balsdean (near Saltdean), 1922. Fokker, seen here in his glider prior to take off, is being towed by the company's Model T-Ford.

119.   An aerial view of Peacehaven, looking north in 1923.

120.   An aerial view of Peacehaven in 1928.

121.   Peacehaven in 1933 looking north-east. Note the bastion steps and the swimming pool on the foreshore. The tides changed the water in the swimming pool twice daily. The water was three to four feet deep. It is also possible to see the chalk circles along the top of the cliff. Before a fence was erected this was the only guide the men, who nightly patrolled the area, had in the dark.

The PRIME MERIDIAN of Greenwich

By Commander W. S. Davenport, R.D., R.N.R. (Retd.)

When the famous writers and poets have exhausted their talent on the wonderful charms of the Sussex Cliffs and Downs, it seems reasonable to ask, " What more can be said ? "

The answer will be found in *The Morning Post*, Sept. 15th, 1933 :

> " The Greenwich Meridian has started a *Risorgimento*
> " in a bungalow town. No other word can convey how . . .
> " Peacehaven, the bungalow garden city, has changed from
> " a timid little resort to the proudest, most geographically
> " minded seaside place in England."

Right here across the green promenade is where the visitor will see where the *Risorgimento* commenced, a broad white strip of stonework some fifty yards long, with a groove running down the middle right down to the very edge of the cliff to mark the exact position of the Prime Meridian that plays a most important part in the subjects of Geography and Astronomy.

At first the visitor is a little curious when he comes to this unique demarcation, and cannot help but wonder what it all means. When was the Prime Meridian established ? To those who have no desire to delve into ancient history we will pass over Eratosthenes, born 270 B.C. Claudius Ptolemæus, born A.D. 150, who in their turn based measurements over the earth from a Prime Meridian.

Let us likewise pass over Ptolemy's great work on geography and a thousand years after. We will even dispense with the voyages of Christopher Columbus, who, as everyone knows, added a great impetus to map and globe making.

Let us, therefore, for the interest of the modern student, commence in 1677 when the Meridian of Greenwich appears to have been first used on our sea charts.

The Royal Observatory, through which the Prime Meridian passes, was founded in 1675 by Charles II, and from that date it has been one of the foremost of the world's observatories from which most ships of the world measured their distances east and west, and from which most countries of the world took their time.

The Standard Mean Time Clock at Greenwich that broadcasts the " six dot seconds " or " pips " is regulated by the astronomer at Greenwich with the Prime Meridian as an index.

Is it not curious that a line, imaginary as it has been, and playing so important a part, should be brought into existence for the first time—except at Greenwich—after so many years.

To produce the line from Pole to Pole its total length measures 10,800 sea miles.

England claims but 174 miles of it, and it would appear to be safe to say that Peacehaven claims more of it than any other place in England.

Space will not permit to describe the Celestial Prime Meridian from which line (the same line extended overhead) the sun, moon, stars and planets are calculated in Declination and Right Ascension.

The visitor cannot fail to be equally interested in the wooden structure temporarily erected astride the line, as will be seen in the illustration on page 23. On the four finger boards or arms will be seen the distances—if not as the crow flies—then certainly as the wireless wave flies, of a few of the most important places in all the five continents.

At the request of the Air Ministry, the exact position of the Prime Meridian at Peacehaven has been marked on the 6 in. aerial map for reference.

When the permanent structure is completed, there is no doubt it will be recorded on all Admiralty Charts, as an additional guide to the mariner.

122. Commander W. S. Davenport (a Peacehaven Councillor) proposed that a committee should be formed to raise money to erect a Meridian Memorial.

123. Initially, a temporary structure was used to promote public interest the final results can be seen on the following pages.

SILVER
YEAR 1935
JUBILEE

To Commemorate the Silver Jubilee of their Most Gracious Majesties King George V. and Queen Mary

and

To mark Peacehaven's interesting position on the Prime Meridian of Greenwich

Peacehaven Unites
in a Ceremony and Fête to Inaugurate the Erection of an
Obelisk and Drinking Fountain
as a Permanent Memorial.

124 & 125.   The programme of events for the celebrations on 10 August 1935. The picture below shows a model of Peacehaven's Silver Jubilee Prime Meridian Memorial. It was taken from a perspective drawing by the Honorary Architect, Mr. R. Jones, L.R.I.B.A.

126.   Peacehaven's Prime Meridian obelisk was unveiled at Peacehaven by Mr. C. W. Neville. The Meridian Queen, seen on the right in all her regalia, was Daphne Poplett. The total cost of the memorial was £300, most raised by subscription, although £100 was guaranteed anonymously.

127 & 128.   In 1800 a line of circles was dug near the cliff edge and infilled with chalk. In pitch dark the coastguards would patrol the promenade, armed with little more than oil lamps and, using the circles as a guide, they kept shipping away from danger. Unfortunately, as no sea protection work had been carried out, three-quarters of the promenade has gradually been allowed to crumble into the sea at a rate of about 18 inches per annum. The new cliff walk has stopped the erosion.

129 & 130.   The Cliff promenade, and in the distance, an Observer Corp Tower built at the start of the Second World War. This was one of many that were built along the south coast, every five to ten miles, manned day and night to detect enemy aircraft. This picture shows a tower being demolished in 1949.

131. Looking west along the promenade in the early 1930s, before the Prime Meridian Memorial was built.

132. Roderick Avenue in 1949. Shortly before this picture was taken a young child had fallen from the unfenced cliffs. There was a public outcry, but the council could not afford to fence off the area. The public took up the challenge and by various means raised money. A thousand pounds was eventually collected, a colossal amount in those days, and the posts and wire subsequently purchased. These old gents put the fence up over one and a quarter miles – 'Great Fellas'.

133. In the 1930s a beach pool was built at the Bastion out of reinforced concrete. The author who worked on its construction, remembers being paid 8d. per hour and often had to work all night whilst the tide was out. The water in the pool was changed every tide. Unfortunately during the Second World War it was neglected and later had to be demolished.

134 & 135.   In 1921, Mr. Neville employed Gordon Volk as a full-time artist. Volk was responsible for designing all the promotional and advertising literature for the estate. Having given Mr. Neville an artist's impression of the Bastion steps, work went ahead. The photograph below shows the completed structure some 50 years later.

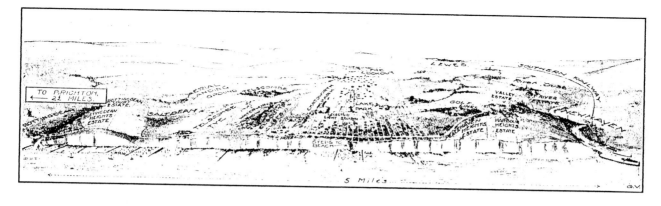

136 & 137. Two bird's-eye views of Peacehaven from Rottingdean to Newhaven. The first picture was drawn by Gordon Volk in the early 1920s and the aerial photograph was taken *c*.1970.

138.   The tennis courts at Saltdean, now the site of the Saltdean Lido which was built in the mid-1930s.

139.   Saltdean Bay in the early 1920s, looking east, when it was part of Greater Peacehaven.

140. A view looking east, at what was to be called Saltdean Estate, 1926.

141. The tearooms at Saltdean in 1926. They were built in the mid-1920s but were demolished during the Second World War.

142. Saltdean Estate in the mid-1930s. What a difference a few years have made!

143. A 1931 aerial view showing Malines Avenue to Telscombe Cliffs Way. As can be seen from the picture, very little remains of the steps that led from Central Avenue to the beach. During the First World War the government had them destroyed to prevent easy access in the event of invasion – a constant threat. The aerodrome was situated in the top half, right-hand side of the picture.

144. An interior view of the Electrical Power Station, in 1922. It was situated at Lincoln Avenue where the airfield hanger once stood. The station was demolished in 1960.

145 & 146. By the 1940s additional machinery had been installed at the power station to cope with the increasing demand for electric lighting. The picture above shows the second diesel oil engine (70 h.p.) driving the generator, and on the left, the booster. The picture on the right shows the supplementary switchboard.

147. A 1923 picture showing the water pumps. They were built by the Peacehaven Water Company at Saltdean Vale, to supply the community with about 120,000 gallons of water a day.

148. In 1921 elevated water tanks were built onto steel towers. The tower in the picture was built on the site of what is now the new school, in Central Avenue, whilst the other tank was at Telscombe. The towers have since been demolished and the water is now transported via underground pipes.

THE PEACEHAVEN POST

Vol. I.
No. 1.

September, 1921.

A JOURNAL OF DOWNLAND
EDITED BY G.H.POWELL

Tea at Peacehaven.

PRICE TWOPENCE

149, 150, 151, 152 & 153.   Four pages from the first edition of the *Peacehaven Post*, dated 1 September 1921. All the drawings were done by Gordon Volk.

FOREWORD

FOREWORD : THE PEACEHAVEN POST is intended to record the doings and developments of the Garden City by the Sea ; keeping subscribers informed upon matters of local interest, and guiding them among the historical, literary, social and other associations of the Downland.

It will be published monthly, and will be obtainable at all the Bookstalls in the neighbourhood, or by post. Annual subscription, four shillings in the United Kingdom.

Original contributions upon matters of interest will be welcomed ; they should be written on one side of the paper only and be accompanied by the name and address of the writer, with stamped addressed envelope for return of unsuitable manuscript.

ADVERTISEMENTS.—Application for rates and spaces vacant should be sent to the Advertisement Manager, THE PEACEHAVEN POST, Peacehaven, near Newhaven, Sussex.

PEACE—Thrice blessed word to hearts that seek
A HAVEN from the storm and stress of life.

ON noble heights swept by the ocean breeze;
    Where eye can take its fill e'en to the brim,
Of Downland glories, mighty banks and leas;
    Mid eerie cries of seagull as they trim
Their wings to kiss the crested wave below;
    Seek ye such gifts that Nature doth bestow?

They are here!   Peacehaven.

A Land of Romance.

View From The "Look Out."

An Eden Environment

THE possibilities of Peacehaven are concerned with the near future. The actualities of Peacehaven lie around us. The least observant eye can realise them. The word " actualities " is, perhaps, not happily chosen, for that which lies around Peacehaven is a Land of Romance.

The new haven by the Sussex sea nestles in the heart of the glorious downs that poets love to sing about and artists love to paint. It is the dreamland that inspired the genius of Rudyard Kipling to its master song :

" Here through the strong and shadeless days
  A tinkling silence thrills ;
Or little, lost, Down churches praise
  The Lord who made the hills.
But here the old Gods guard their round,
  And in her secret heart
The heathen-kingdom Wilfrid found
  Dreams, as she dwells, apart."

We may dream apart in Peacehaven, but while we dream the Land of Romance that lies around would tempt us to survey its beauties and surrender ourselves to its charms.

Peacehaven is an admirable starting point for exploring the Wonderland of which it is the happy centre, the glories of the green hills, the pastoral charms of the hidden valleys that the old Gods still guard in dreamland's secret heart.

In the pages of THE PEACEHAVEN POST we propose from time to time to tell the story of these old-world beauty spots that knew the ancient woad-stained Britons, that saw the Saxons and knew the Norman conquerors, and have survived, almost unchanged, to become the happy haunts of the people of an England upon the dominions of whose Sovereign the sun never sets.

It is a reproach to many well-to-do Englishmen that they know other people's countries better than their own. There may be men of Sussex who have but little knowledge of the wonderful story that is to be found in the picturesque pages of the glorious green volume that bears the title of " Downland."

It is a verdant volume whose pages enshrine some of the most stirring and romantic incidents in English history. Many of these will be narrated again in the pages of THE PEACEHAVEN POST. They will be told, as it were, " on the spot," for we shall take our readers to the historic towns, to the ancient homes of British kings, to the crumbling castles grown grey with age, to old-world villages and to quaint old churches, some of them dating almost from the commencement of the Christian faith among the dwellers in Downland.

We shall wander with them over flowering meads and seek the hidden havens of the hills. Our readers will go with us to favoured spots along the sunny shores that have grown from little fishing hamlets into breezy boroughs by the brine, health and pleasure resorts of world-wide fame.

We shall wander the by-ways of Sussex, those by-ways of peace and beauty that William Blake, poet and painter and seer, roamed in a mystic mood that enables you—

" To see a World in a Grain of Sand,
  And a Heaven in a Wild Flower ;
Hold Infinity in the palm of your hand,
  And Eternity in an hour."

In our happy pilgrimage, we shall pause awhile to survey the panorama of pastoral peace

154. A poster, drawn by Gordon Volk, advertising Peacehaven in 1921. The railway never did come to Peacehaven, but advertising literature continued the theme to make people think that one day it would.

PRINTING ORDERS are **Promptly Executed** at the "Gazette" Works.

PEACEHAVEN & NEWHAVEN
AND SOUTH COAST
Gazette

"Gazette" Advertising is **Efficient** and **Cheap.**

Send for Rates.

No. 253. | (Registered at the G.P.O. as a Newspaper.) | Established March, 1924. | SATURDAY, JAN. 12. 1929. | Fourth Year of Publication | Telephone Peacehaven **21** | Price 1d.

The Kenya Club.

In connection with the R.A.O.B., G.S.B., Lodge and the Kenya Club an open evening was held on the club premises on Friday, Dec. 30. Several members contributed to the programme, among them visitors and members from Newhaven and Seaford. Bro. Barker, K.O.M. presided supported by his officers.

On New Year's night a very jolly time was spent by a good number of members and friends, at a dance and social evening.

Wanted!

Owing to the death of a very valued public servant employed by the Parish Council, a successor is required to fulfill the duties of lamp-lighter, cleaning the shelters, etc. Applicants for this post should apply to the Chairman of the Parish Council, Mr. A. Harrison, at The Downs Library, South Coast-road.

THE PEOPLE'S MARKET
Is the Store for You—Full Value ever.

Ridgway's, Brooke's, Lyons', Mazawattee, Doctor's and Typhoo Teas.

Delicious Butter	... ...	1/10
New-laid Eggs	... doz.	2/0
Peaches	... tin	10½d.
Fruit Salad	... lb	1/-
Apricots	... lb.	1/-
Apple Rings	... lb.	1/-
2's Black current and Apple		10½d.
2's Apricot	...	1/1
2's Raspberry	...	1/3
2's Strawberry	...	1/4
2's Marmalade	...	10½d.

SHOP EARLY!

WINKWORTH & SON,
Central Stores,
SOUTH COAST ROAD,

155. The *Peacehaven & Newhaven Gazette*, Saturday, 12 January 1929.

156. The first edition of the *Peacehaven & Newhaven Times*, 13 December 1946.

Peacehaven & Newhaven
Times

Registered at the G.P.O. as a Newspaper

No. 1. FRIDAY, 13th DECEMBER, 1946

Twopence

ALSO CIRCULATING IN SALTDEAN, ROTTINGDEAN

CONDITIONS in SQUATTERS' CAMP

LACK OF LABOUR CAUSES DISCOMFORT

About 40 families are still living in the huts of Rushy Hill Camp, Newhaven Heights, with little chance of being found better accommodation for some considerable time. Conditions there are as good as can be expected in such an exposed position, and would be much improved if the Council had the necessary labour available to carry out conversions.

Materials

Many of the huts still have no partitions, but there is plenty of material, and some tenants are carrying out their own improvements, with material supplied by the Council.

In this way many of the huts have been made fairly comfort-

other facilities, such as gas, for cooking, the Council hope to get permission from the Minister of Fuel for an extra allocation of coal and coke for the camp.

Lighting and Rent

All the huts are supplied with electric light, for which a charge of 2/6d per week is made. This

CHILD KNOCKED DOWN BY CAR

An accident occurred at the junction of Broomfield Ave. and South Peacehaven, on Tuesday afternoon.

Patricia Bird, aged 7, of

NEWHAVEN PORT

"Times" Reporter Visits the Harbour

Newhaven must remain bomb scarred, and the administration must still function from their "hole in the corner" offices as long as Housing remains No. 1 priority. The time when the Port's buildings will be made fittingly modern, is as far distant as it was in 1938. This delay, nevertheless, may be to the ultimate good of the Port if the re-building is postponed until controls are completely removed, then we may see

Saltdean Amenities

"It is high time that some attempt was made to make Saltdean a little less like a wilderness." This statement was made to a "Times" representative by a local resident, who went on to say that a great number of people were dissatisfied with the lack of local amenities, and that a large number of houses would be empty if the general housing position were not so acute.

Restricted 'bus services, the absence of a cinema and pub., were among many other points raised.

Saltdean, he continued, was no longer the Mecca of well to do week-enders, but a normal community living in a com

157. In 1922 horse-drawn transport was very popular, as you long as you did not get stuck in the mud! The two men seen in the picture are Mr. Cartright the land agent and his ostler.

158.   Mr. Ernest Facks, seen here with his horse named Major, operated the first private rubbish collection service between 1920 and 1934. In 1934 the council made a compulsory purchase order and took over the service, but employed the previous employees of Mr. Facks, as well as Mr. Facks and Major.

159.   The imposing *Castle Hotel*, built on the South Coast Road near Bramber Avenue in 1922.

PEACEHAVEN BRANCH.

GRAND ANNUAL

FETE & SPORTS

ON THE

PROMENADE

(Between Piddinghoe and Gladys Avenues).

On Monday, August 3rd,

Commencing at **2.30 p.m**.

2.30 Opening Ceremony
2 to 5.30 Races for all
2.30 to 4—5.30 to 7 Boxing Tournament
7 to 7.30 Distribution of Prizes and Medals
7.30 to 8.30 Pierrot Entertainment
8.30 to 10 p.m. Dancing

Bands !   Side Shows ! !   Novelties ! ! !

Lucky Number Programmes **2d.**

**TEAS AND REFRESHMENTS at Popular
Prices.**

160.   British Legion brochure for 3 August 1931. The local branch of the Legion was formed in the early 1920s. Events such as this played an important part in the social life of the community.

Combine a comfortable car, an experienced driver
and low rates with your

CAR   JOURNEYS.

These can all be assured by engaging

W. R. HURMAN,

Daimler Hire Car and Taxi
Proprietor.

ALDERSHOT   TATTOO
AND
ASCOT   RACES.

W. R. HURMAN will be running parties of six passengers
to these Meetings   TARIFF ON APPLICATION.

Ring up Peacehaven 9, or apply :

TAXI STATION, HODDERN AVENUE,
PEACEHAVEN.

Peacehaven Press, Peacehaven.

161.   An advertisement for car and taxi hire, 1927.
Mr. Hurman, an early pioneer and resident of
Peacehaven set up the taxi company. Unfortunately the
business did not prosper, so Mr. Hurman closed it down
and became a coal-man.

Bannister & Sons, Ltd.,

NEWHAVEN.

SEASONABLE LINES.

BLUE PEAS	3d. and 4d. per lb.	
HARICOT BEANS	1½d. ,, ,,
BUTTER BEANS	3d. ,, ,,
BURMA BEANS	2d. ,, ,,
OATMEALS (all oats)	2½d. ,, ,,
ROLLED OATS	2½d. ,, ,,
RANGOON RICE	2½d. ,, ,,
SPANISH JAPAN RICE	3½d. ,, ,,
GROUND RICE	3d. ,, ,,

DAILY DELIVERY TO PEACEHAVEN.

Terms : Cash.

Post Orders receive Special Attention.

New Cereal Price List.

Rolled Oats
Oatmeal
Rice — **2d.** Per lb.
Split Peas
Pearl Barley — **7 lbs. for**
Haricot Beans — **1/1**

7 lb. Empire Flour - - 9d.
3 lb. Empire S.R. Flour - - 5d.

We heve many lines below market value.

Now is the time to Buy.

Pay us a Visit—and buy British.

SARGEANT'S LTD.,

High Street & Chapel Street,
NEWHAVEN. Phone 64.

162, 163, 164 & 165. Advertisements and receipts from a variety of business that operated in Peacehaven, in the 1920s and 30s. Note the cost of the items such as oatmeal at 2½d. – about one penny in today's money!

Mr Rodhouse

Dr. to ...

YE OLDE ROSEMARY DAIRY

AND TEA GARDENS.

PEACEHAVEN.

'PHONE 77. PROPRIETOR: A. J. BAGNALL.

Week ending ......1934.							£	s.	d.
Amount brought forward ...								6	0
	Sun.	Mon.	Tues.	Wed.	Thurs.	Fri.	Sat.		
Milk									
Nursery Milk	✓	✓	✓	✓	✓	✓	✓		2	7
Cream									
Butter									
New-Laid Eggs									
						Total £		8	7

"THE LAURELS." CISSBURY AVENUE.
CLIFF PARK, NEWHAVEN.

Mr F. G. Rodhouse ...... Nov 1st 1935

Dr. to **E. FACKS,**

CARMAN AND CONTRACTOR.

CESSPITS EMPTIED. REFUSE COLLECTED.

TERMS: Cash on completion of order.

Order Number		Hours	Rate	£	s.	d.
	Castle Restaurant					
	exp. Reddived.			1	4	c

RECEIPT.   No. HII 775

The South Coast Land and Resort Company.

Received of *Albert Ernest Harley Esq.*

of *"Holmleigh" Albany Road, Coventry, Warwickshire*

the Sum of *Four Guineas* (*£4/4/-*) being payment in full for

a Building Plot at New ~~Anzac-on-Sea~~ *Peacehaven*, which is to include a Deed

of Conveyance with the Government Stamp Duty paid.

For and behalf of

THE SOUTH COAST LAND AND RESORT COMPANY.

£4 : 4 :    *Secretary.*

Date 3 MAR 1917

NOTE.—The usual time for the preparation and completion of a Deed of Conveyance is about thirty days. The Deed will be forwarded to you by registered post immediately it is returned to us from Somerset House duly stamped.

No. 0338   TEMPORARY RECEIPT.

South Coast Land & Resort Co., Ltd.
PEACEHAVEN, SUSSEX.
London Office: 4 VERNON PLACE, BLOOMSBURY, W.C. 1.

1. 3. 1922

Received of *G. F. Rodhouse Esq.*

the sum of *ten pounds -*

being the Amount paid in respect to the Purchase of Plots *36, 37,*

in Block *12* PEACEHAVEN ESTATE.

For and on behalf of SOUTH COAST LAND & RESORT CO., LTD.

W. Langelin

£10 : . : .   STAMP   *Agent.*

No. 8100

South Coast Land & Resort Co., Ltd.
4 VERNON PLACE, BLOOMSBURY. W.C.1.

10 - 2 1923

Received of *G F Rodhouse Esq*

the sum of *Nine pounds*

being the Amount paid in respect to the Purchase of ~~Plots~~

in Block *1. 2757 6* PEACEHAVEN ESTATE.

For and on behalf of SOUTH COAST LAND & RESORT CO., LTD.

£9 : — : —   *Wb.*   *Cashier.*

WITH THANKS.

JORDAN AND SONS, LIMITED, CHANCERY LANE, W.C.2—3311

166, 167 & 168.   The freehold price of three plots of land in March 1917, March 1922 and February 1923. The price for 100 ft. x 25 ft. started as low as £4 to £5 per plot, depending on the location. Plots on the main road could go for as much as £100 to £150.

OFFICIAL PROGRAMME

OF

PEACEHAVEN'S

Coronation

Celebrations

With Order of the United Service

TO COMMEMORATE
THE CORONATION OF

Their Majesties

King George VI. & Queen Elizabeth

MAY 12th, 1937.

PRICE 2D.

169. An official programme advertising the Peacehaven Coronation celebrations, 1937. The festivities began with a procession which started at Steyning Avenue at 10.30 a.m. and ended up at the Amphitheatre – now the Dell – where a service was held.

CHAILEY RURAL DISTRICT COUNCIL

A. F. PERKINS
CLERK AND
SUPERINTENDENT REGISTRAR
OF LEWES REGISTRATION DISTRICT

TELEPHONES {698
{699

IN REPLY PLEASE QUOTE 257

YOUR REFERENCE ....

31. HIGH STREET,

LEWES

SECRET.

22nd October 1941.

Dear Sir,

Feeding of Home Guard in Case of an Invasion.

I beg to inform you that I have given authority for the supply of rationed foods to the Home Guard when they are ordered to muster for the purposes of resisting an invasion.

In some cases it may be felt that the Retailer's stocks might prove insufficient to meet the demands made upon them for Home Guard purposes. Retailers are allowed to carry stocks of certain rationed foods which should, in general, be sufficient to meet the immediate requirements of the Home Guard when mustered. If you are satisfied that your stocks will prove insufficient for this purpose and you can carry and turn over an increased stock, maintaining it on that footing in readiness for use in due course for Home Guard purposes, I am at liberty to issue a supplementary permit to you to enable this to be done. The weekly amounts of the commodities which I have given orders for from you are as follows:-

	Weekly Amounts	
Bacon/Ham	18	lbs
Butter	9	"
Margarine	22½	"
Cooking Fats	18	"
Tea	9	"
Sugar	31½	"
Preserves	18	"

Yours faithfully,

A. F. Perkins

Food Executive Officer.

Messrs. Sayers,
Roderick Avenue,
Peacehaven.

170. A letter from Chailey Rural District Council, concerning feeding of the Home Guard in case of an invasion, 1941.

WOMEN'S INSTITUTE
FLOWER
AND PRODUCE
SHOW
WEDNESDAY, JULY 26TH

ST. PHILOMENA'S
CONVENT SCHOOL,
EDITH AVENUE

TO BE OPENED AT 2.45 p.m. BY
MISS LILIAN MARTIN

PRIZE DISTRIBUTION AT 6.30 p.m. BY
MRS. CORNELIUS

Admission by Lucky Programme 3d.   Children at door 1d.

TELSCOMBE
AND DISTRICT
HORTICULTURAL SOCIETY
FIRST SUMMER
SHOW
WEDNESDAY, AUG. 2ND
AT
TELSCOMBE HALL
(OFF BROOMFIELD AVENUE)

OPENING CEREMONY 2.30 p.m.

PRIZEGIVING AT 5.30 p.m. BY
MISS ALICE KIRKBY

Admission 4d. Children 1d.   Teas & Refreshments

PEACEHAVEN, TELSCOMBE & DISTRICT
FUR, FEATHER &
HORTICULTURAL SOCIETY
THIRTEENTH ANNUAL SUMMER
SHOW
FLOWERS & PRODUCE
WILL BE HELD AT
ST. PHILOMENA'S
CONVENT SCHOOL, EDITH AVENUE, on
WEDNESDAY, AUGUST 16TH

TO BE OPENED AT 3 p.m. BY
MRS. A. B. SOMERS

PRIZE DISTRIBUTION AT 6.30 p.m. BY
MRS. W. M. V. PICKARD-CAMBRIDGE

Admission by Lucky Numbered Programme 6d. If purchased before the day 4d.
Children 3d. at Door

171.   Pre-1940 show posters. Fur, Feather and Horticultural Societies were always very well supported and reflect the extent to which people produced their own food – vegetables, eggs, poultry etc.

172.   An article from *The Downland Review*, 1959 with the cast of *The Little House*. There were a great many music hall entertainers who had an attachment to Peacehaven including George Robey, Sandy Powell, Tommy Fields, Harry Tate, Jimmy Wheeler, Flora Robson, Dougie Wakefield, Dick Tubb, Max Wall, Bill Pertwee (fifth from the left), Bill Owen (second from left), Gert & Daisy (Walters), and three world billiard champions; Melbourne Inman, Joe Davis and Horace Lindrum.

Opening of The Little House on January 24th, showing Mr. Colin Gordon and Mr. Percy Edwards (Birdman) both of 'Life of Bliss' programme; Bill Owen and Edith Stevenson (Stars of T.V.); and centre Miss Raymonde-Hawkins and Veterinary Surgeon, with residents' dog as first patient.   *Photo: Sussex Express*

Opening of

THE LITTLE HOUSE

South Coast Road

173 & 174. An account of Peacehaven would not be complete without mentioning a good friend of mine and also of Peacehaven, 'our Gracie', Gracie Fields. Gracie helped her father, Fred Stansfield, to buy a small bungalow in Dorothy Avenue for his retirement, early in 1927. A few years later Gracie bought 'The Haven' at Telscombe Cliffs for her parents and for herself when she was 'resting'. She also helped to set up The Variety Artists Benevolent Fund Orphanage for the children of artists who had fallen on hard times. In the photograph, the right-hand side of the house, with the darker tiled roof, is the area where Fred Stansfield lived; the left-hand side of the building was built on at a later date. The building now serves as an old people's home.

175. Harry Poplett (1885-1963), well-known pioneer tradesman.

Final Word

Thank you, dear reader, for reading my book, which I hope you enjoyed. If this is the case please tell others, if not please tell me!

I hope it gave you an insight into the youthful history of Peacehaven, and like me, makes you feel proud for the pioneers, and the founder Mr. C. W. Neville, who helped it to happen.

From gorse and grass covered fields to a thriving town and community, this is truly a 'Garden City by the Sea'.

176.   This tablet in the parish churchyard, commemorates the fallen heroes of the Second World War and the sons of the pioneers of Peacehaven.

IN REMEMBRANCE OF
THE MEN OF PEACEHAVEN WHO DIED ON ACTIVE SERVICE
1939 - 1945

LEONARD ASHTON
HARRY BASHFORD
JOHN BRADLEY
SIDNEY BRIX
WILLIAM CLASEN
MERVYN DAVIES
JOHN DEMPSTER
THEODORE DUNNING
CHARLES FORSYTH

RONALD GARDNER
GEORGE GARMAN
SAMUEL GILLETT
ERNEST HARMAN
PHILIP HARMAN
JOHN HORTON
PETER HURMAN
RICHARD LEE

BRIAN LUCAS
WILLIAM PUTTOCK
LAURENCE RAY
DAVID SELBY-LOWNDES
EDWARD SHAYLER
VERNON STEVENS
ALAN TUCKNOTT
EBENEZER VOAKES
SYDNEY WARD

AND ALL WHO FELL IN THE GREAT WARS

COME TO
PEACEHAVEN
THE GARDEN CITY BY THE SEA